The Little Book of Photography

for DIGITAL and FILM
SLR cameras

Tips, Terms and Techniques
for the Beginner to SLR Photography

J.H. Barnard

Third Edition

Third Edition February 2005

Published in the UK by AllyBoy Books.

Printed by Antony Rowe Ltd.

ISBN 0-9542178-4-5

Cover design by J.H. Barnard
Drawings and photographs by J.H. Barnard

About this book...

This book is for the beginner to SLR photography. It allows you to 'dip' into when you need to know more about a particular term, technique or photographic assignment.

The book is divided into four sections. The first section contains the terms behind SLR photography such as exposure, focussing, focal length and the features found on film and digital SLR cameras. The next section contains typical SLR equipment and accessories such as lenses, filters, camera supports and reflectors and when to use them.
The next two sections look at photographic technique. The first of the two sections describes some common techniques such as how to take silhouettes, apply soft focus, bracketing and when to use the Rule of Thirds.
The final section forms the bulk of book and contains tips for various photographic assignments. Obvious assignments are covered in detail: landscapes, portraits, action and still-life. Other, less known assignments, are also featured, such as wildlife, water, buildings, close-ups, the moon, fireworks and black and white photography. Each assignment is presented as a series of 'bullet points', such as what lens to use, advice on aperture and shutter speed, whether to use a filter, the best time of day to take the shot and so on.

The book is applicable to both film and digital SLR cameras and should be used in conjunction with your SLR camera manual – both are small enough to fit into your camera bag.

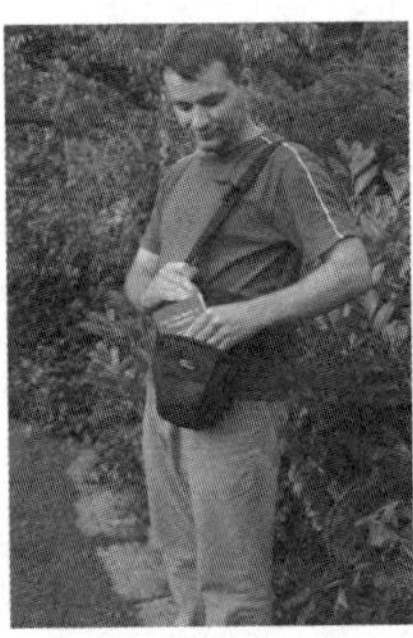

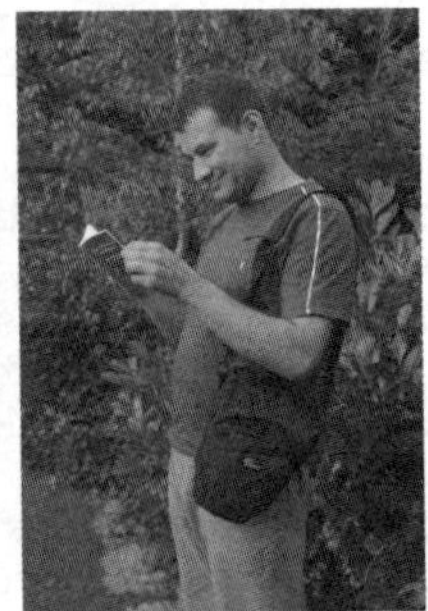

The book has been published by AllyBoy Books, which can be visited at **www.littlephotobook.com**

10p from each book sold is donated to the charity Woodland Trust - the UK's leading conservation charity dedicated to the protection of our native woodland heritage. They can be visited at **www.woodland-trust.org.uk.**

First of all...

... A brief history of photography

All cameras have five basic components:

- A **lens** to focus light rays of an image on film.
- A **film** at the back of the camera to record the image.
- An **aperture** (hole) through which light enters the camera, the size of which can be controlled so that just the right amount of exposure is given to the film.
- A **shutter** that covers the film until the photograph is ready to be taken.
- A **viewfinder** to let the photographer know what he or she is taking.

These components are finely tuned in today's cameras. However they started very simply in the early days of photography: the **camera obscura**, which has been in existence since ancient times, is a darkened room where images are formed on a plate opposite a tiny 'pinhole'. The pinhole lets in light and forms an inverted image of the world outside.

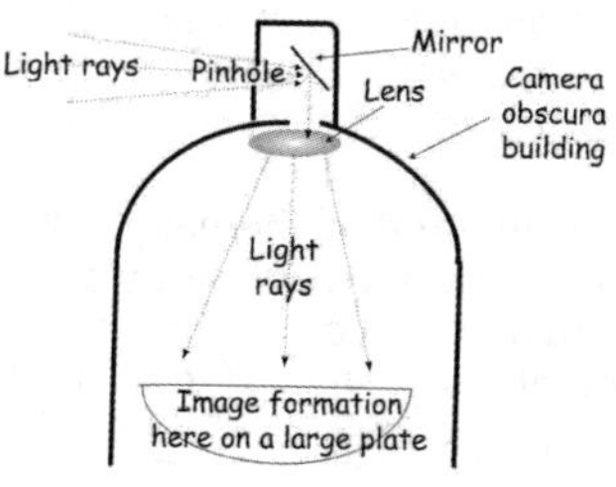

The Camera Obscura

Camera obscura literally means 'dark room'. They use the same principle of image formation as that in the **pinhole camera**.

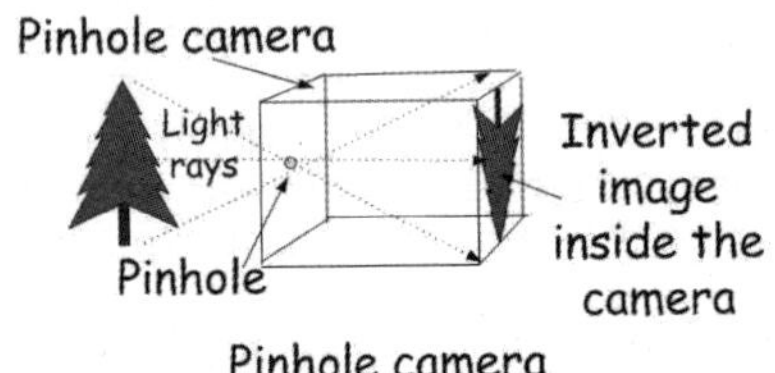

Pinhole camera

The camera obscura was used by artists who would trace the images onto paper and material. In the 17th century, lenses from telescopes were installed into camera obscuras to obtain images with greater clarity.
Early wooden **box cameras** in the 19th century, based on the camera obscura, created images on a plate of ground glass inside the camera. Most cameras of this time were made of mahogany and brass with plates in the back for inserting paper, glass or metal to capture the image. Exposure times for these cameras were often in the region of minutes, later improved by the use of silver compounds.
Roll film was invented in the early 20th century and paved the way for popular photography.
Camera technology moved on with the introduction of plastic mouldings. Cameras in which the bellows folded away into the case made them light and portable.

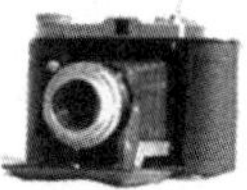

The advances in camera technology was somewhat due to companies in Japan such as Pentax, Canon and Nikon and in Germany, the Leitz and Zeiss companies.

The latter part of the 20th century saw the introduction of the **SLR (Single Lens Reflex) camera** and later the **automatic camera**.

The 21st century has seen the success of the first **digital SLR cameras** with digital film resolutions matching those of conventional film SLR cameras (to the naked eye). Images are stored digitally and can be manipulated very easily using a computer.

It looks increasing likely that the future of photography will reside in the digital world. It has many advantages including the increased speed of photo production, the elimination of chemical processes, image manipulation without the need for a darkroom and the ability to send images quickly over computer networks.

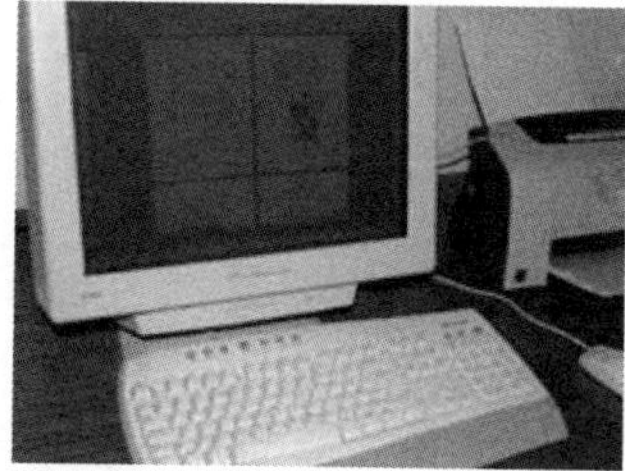

CONTENTS

SLR Camera Terms	11
SLR Camera Accessories	65
Photographic Techniques	89
Photographic Assignments	107
Index	159

SLR Camera Terms

Introduction

The **Single Lens Reflex** (SLR) camera enables you to take photographs with a far greater control than if you used an automatic camera. The SLR camera allows you to take control over things like exposure, how much of the photograph is in focus, special effects (using filters, for example) as well as allowing a wide choice of lenses to be attached to the camera.

Original film SLR cameras look a bit like the one in the diagram below.

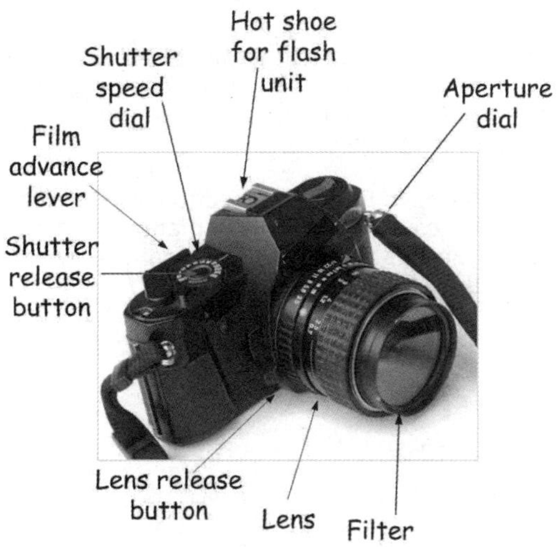

On the whole these cameras require *manual* intervention by the photographer, such as winding on the film with the film advance lever, the focussing mechanism and the setting of the ISO film speed.

Nowadays cameras are built with *electronics*, which automate many of the manual processes. Auto-focus is commonplace, as is the ability to read the ISO film speed of your film without the need for manual input. Built in flash units are commonplace too.

Many of the cameras have facilities such as a self-timer, exposure compensation and pre-programmed mode settings for landscape, portrait, action and close-up photography.

Digital SLRs have been designed to look the same as their film counterparts. Many manufacturers allow their lenses to be used interchangeably between their film and digital models.

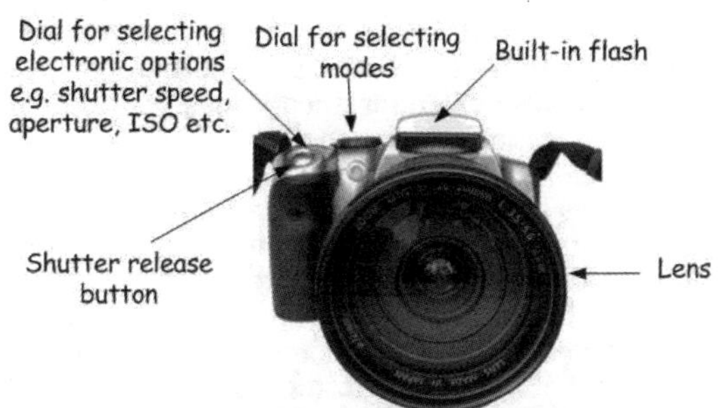

Front view of a typical digital or film SLR camera

The diagram above shows some typical features of a modern film or digital SLR. Your particular camera will have a manufacturer's manual. It is important that you use this manual in conjunction with this book as each model has its own special characteristics, all of which cannot be covered in a book of this style.

The main difference with a digital SLR is the use of a memory card rather than inserting film. The card stores the photographs you take electronically. You are able to delete these photos if you wish or transfer them to a computer. Additionally digital SLRs have a LCD screen on the back of the camera allowing the photographer to view their photograph instantaneously. This has many benefits - it allows the photographer to check their photograph before they print it out. If they have made a mistake or the photo is not quite how they expected then they simply delete it and try again. This saves time and resources. Being able to see your photograph immediately after taking it encourages you to improve your photography too.

SLR cameras have slots for the battery, memory card (if digital) and also some cable sockets (for a remote switch and, if digital, to connect to your computer). It is a good idea to have two batteries - whilst one is recharging you can use the other. Ideally you should have two memory cards with your digital SLR - nothing would be worse if you filled up your memory card whilst on holiday without a spare one for further photos.

The typical components of the rear of a digital SLR are shown below.

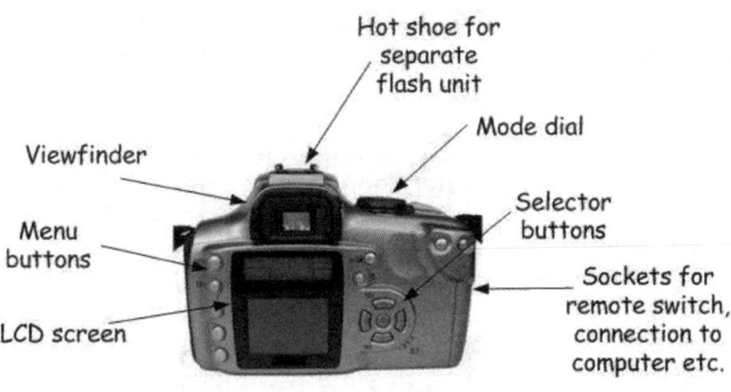

Rear view of a typical digital SLR camera

The SLR Camera

The **Single Lens Reflex** (SLR) camera is so called because it uses the same (single) lens for forming an image in the viewfinder (i.e. what the photographer sees) and for forming an image on the film. The light from the lens is reflected up to the viewfinder-focussing screen by a **reflex mirror**. When you fully depress the shutter release button (i.e. when you take a picture), the mirror swings up to let the light pass to the film at the back of the camera.

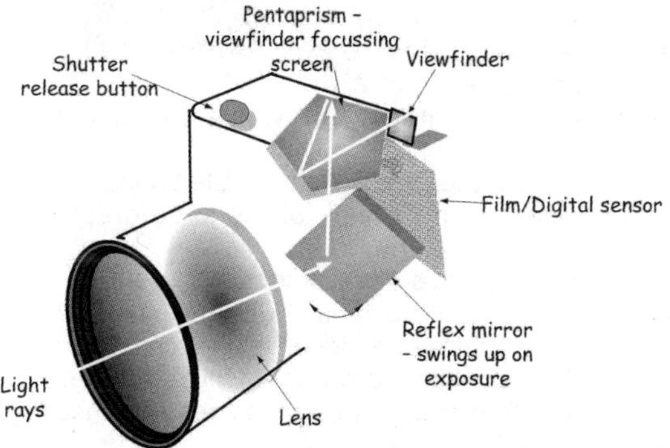

Internal components of an SLR camera

When you look through the viewfinder of an SLR camera you are seeing exactly what the film will record. This is known as **TTL (Through-The-Lens)** focusing.

Lenses

A lens is a specially designed piece of optical glass that collects and focuses rays of light from an object to form a sharp image. The point at which the light rays meet is called the **focal point**. If camera film is placed at the focal point, a sharp image is formed on the film.

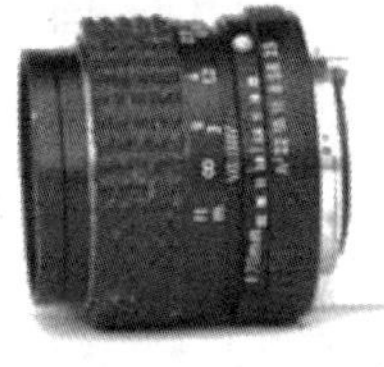

The lens is the most important part of the camera. It is generally thought that it is better to have an expensive lens on a cheap camera body than to have an expensive camera body, with lots of features, but with a cheap lens.

You need to buy the best lens possible as the lens plays a big part in the quality of the photograph.

You may want to have several lenses in your collection to cater for various situations, such as landscapes, portraits and close-ups. Alternatively one zoom lens covering a range of focal lengths may suit you. See the section on Types of Lenses (pages 66-68) for further details.

Focussing

Focussing
Focussing involves turning the lens so that a sharp image is displayed on the film or digital sensor plane. As already mentioned, TTL focussing means that you view exactly what the film will record.

Most SLR cameras these days employ an auto-focus facility as well as a manual focus.

Manual focus
Manual focussing involves turning the focusing ring of the lens until a sharp image can be viewed in the viewfinder. Some older cameras use **split-image focussing** in which the image viewed is split in two and focussing involves lining up the two parts.

Autofocus
Autofocus is a mechanism in which the camera uses techniques based on the contrasts and edges of objects being photographed in order to achieve a correctly focussed image. On most SLR cameras, pressing the shutter release button down halfway triggers the autofocus.
There are some situations where autofocus may not work, such as scenes where there is little contrast, such as a plain blue sky, or in low light conditions, in which case it is best to adjust your camera to use manual focus.

Focussing points

In the basic autofocus mode the camera tends to focus on whatever is in the centre of the frame. However there are times when you want to select which part of the photograph is in focus *yourself*. By manually selecting a focussing point, you can ensure that a certain object or part of a photograph is in sharp focus. This is known as *manual* autofocus point selection.

Through the viewfinder the focussing points are usually displayed like that shown below. You can select any of the points depending on which part of the photograph they cover and whether you want that part in focus. In this photograph the photographer wants the post in sharp focus. However this is to the left of the scene and so the focussing point shown is the one selected.

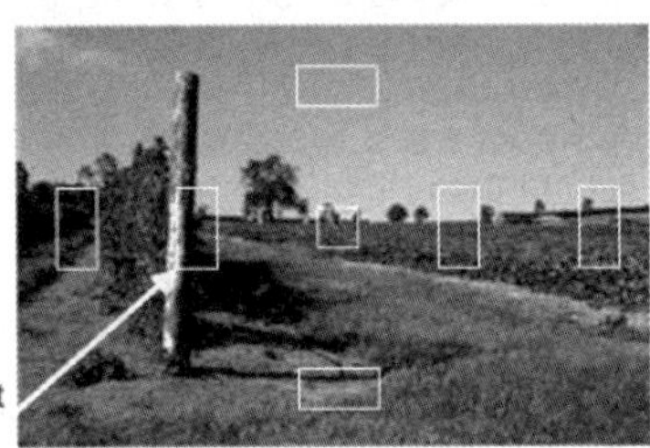

Select this focussing point to ensure the post is in sharp focus

In *automatic* autofocus point selection mode, the camera focuses on the *nearest* object.

Focus lock

An alternative to using focussing points (or if your camera does not support multiple focussing points) is focus lock. Considering the photograph on the previous page, the photographer looks through the viewfinder with the post in the *centre* then focuses on it (using autofocus with the shutter release button depressed halfway). With the shutter release button stlll depressed, the photographer recomposes the photograph i.e. with the post to the left, and then takes the photograph.

Focus lock is also useful in situations where autofocus is having problems – such as in low contrast or lowlight conditions. By focussing on an object the same distance away, then employing focus lock and recomposing the photograph, you will overcome this problem.

Depth of focus

The depth of focus refers to the distance (often very tiny) over which a film could be shifted inside the camera with the subject remaining in focus. It is a term that you are unlikely to use and should not be confused with the term *depth of field*.

Focal Length

The **focal length** of a lens is the distance between the lens and the film when the lens is focussed on a distant subject.

Different lenses can have different focal lengths. If a lens has a focal length of 200mm it would be known as a '200mm lens'.

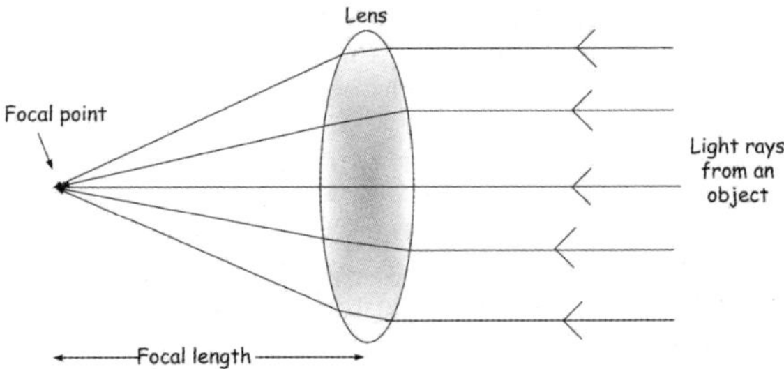

For photographic assignments the recommended lenses are usually as follows:

- Wide-angle lens (in the region 17–35 mm) are best for landscapes.
- Lenses with a focal length of around 100mm are good for portraits.
- For wildlife photography in which subjects are often distant, a telephoto lens (in the range 100-400mm) would be required.

Clearly a zoom lens with a range of say 20-300mm would enable the photographer to use it in a variety of assignments. This is one of the reasons why

zoom lenses are more popular than lenses of fixed focal length.
The physical length of a lens is generally related to its focal length – the longer the focal length, the longer the lens.

The longer the focal length, the larger the subject appears. So a 200mm lens records a subject much larger (magnified) than a 35mm lens at the same distance from the subject. The angle of view (see page 25) is the term for the amount a lens 'sees' and is related to the focal length.

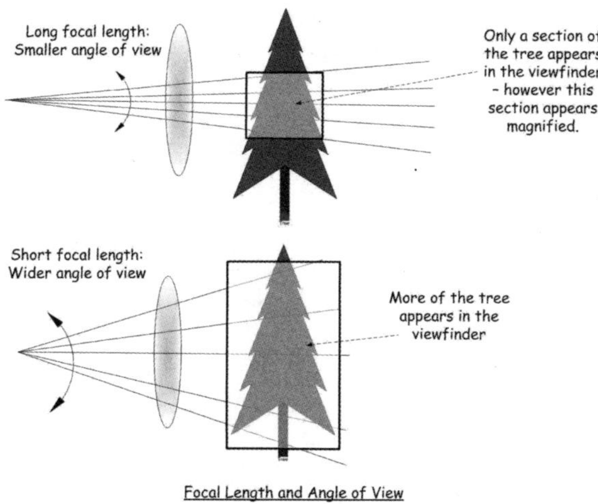

Focal Length and Angle of View

Lens speed
Lenses are often expressed in terms of their focal length e.g. 35mm-80mm and also by an f-number or an f-number range. The f-number in this case is the maximum aperture setting (smallest f-number) that the lens can achieve.
The lens speed is related to this maximum aperture. The smaller the maximum aperture of a lens, the 'slower' the lens. A 'fast' lens has a larger maximum aperture, so an f/1.4 lens is faster than an f/2.8 lens. For more information on aperture see page 27.

Angle of view
The 'angle of view' (i.e. how wide a view the lens can capture) is related to the focal length and is smaller for longer focal lengths, whereas lenses with shorter focal lengths have a wider angle of view.
A wide-angle lens, therefore, has a wide angle of view and a short focal length e.g. 20mm. It is unable to provide any significant magnification of a distant subject. It is useful in landscape photography.
A telephoto lens, on the other hand, has a small angle of view but is able to provide magnification of a distant subject. A typical focal length of a telephoto lens is 200mm. It is useful for close-ups of distant objects such as in wildlife photography.

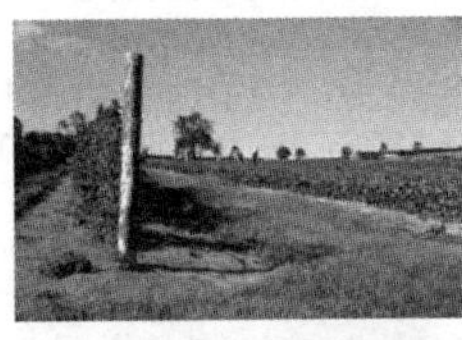

A photograph with a wide angle of view (taken with a 28mm focal length lens)

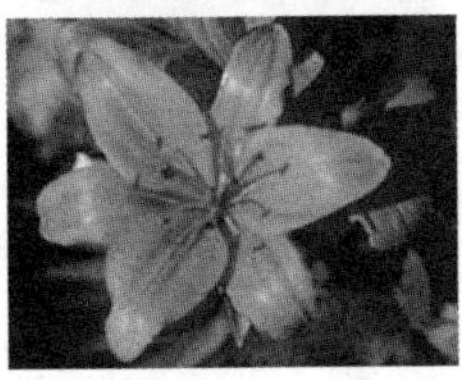

A photograph with a narrow angle of view (taken with a 200mm focal length lens)

Aperture and Shutter Speed

Taking a photograph requires the lens to focus the light rays on the camera film/digital sensor. It also requires that the light entering the camera be controlled so that the image is not over-exposed (appears lighter) or under-exposed (appears darker). Controlling the amount of light is done *primarily* through two mechanisms: the size of the hole through which the light enters (called the **aperture**) and also the length of time that the film is exposed to this light (controlled by the **shutter speed**).
Taking a correctly exposed photograph requires that you have the correct combination of aperture and shutter speed. There can be many combinations that will give you a correctly exposed photograph: the one you choose depends on how you want the photograph to look.

Put simply, a wide aperture will require a shorter shutter speed, whereas a small aperture will require a longer exposure.

Other things can be used to affect how your photograph is exposed, such as the film speed, the type of lighting, using a flash or using filters. These will be looked at in later sections of the book.

Aperture

Aperture is the opening in the lens where light enters. It controls the amount of light entering the camera. It also affects the depth of field (page 28). Its size is expressed as an f-number.
A low f-number (e.g. f/2.8 – see diagram below) is a large aperture that lets in more light than a small one. A high f-number (e.g. f/22 – see diagram below) is a small aperture that lets in less light. Typical f-numbers that cameras support are f/1.4, f/2, f/2.8, f/4, f/5.6, f/8, f/11, f/16 and f/22.

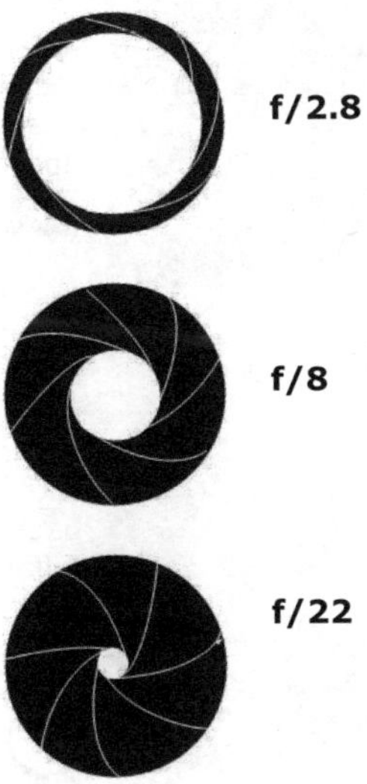

Depth of field

Depth of field relates to the amount of a photograph that is in focus. You can change the depth of field by adjusting the aperture, but it is also affected by the magnification of your lens and the distance that the camera is from the subject.

More information on Depth of Field can be found on page 92.

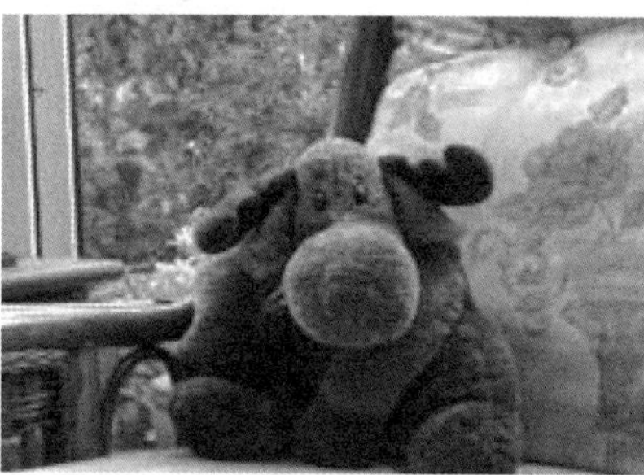

Large depth of field - the toy and the background foliage are in focus. (Narrow aperture -f/22)

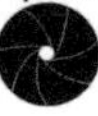

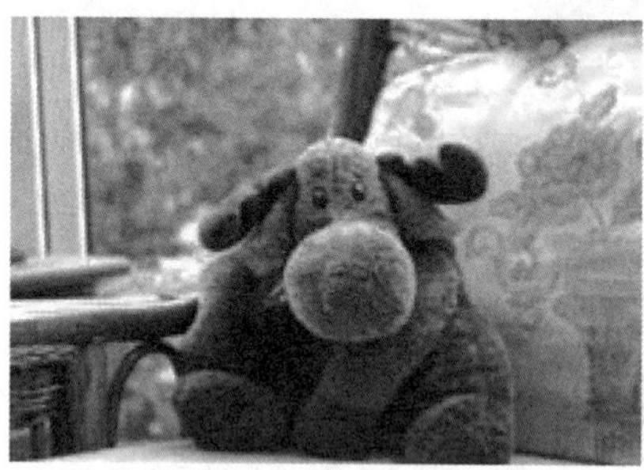

Small depth of field - only the toy is in focus with the background foliage out of focus. (Wide aperture -f/4.0)

Shutter speed

The shutter speed is not actually a speed at all but the length of time that the film is exposed to light.

A high shutter speed (e.g. 1/500th second) lets in less light to the film and is good for freezing action shots.

A lower shutter speed (e.g. 1/10th second) lets in more light to the film and is useful in low light conditions, but if objects are moving they can appear blurred.

Typical shutter speeds that cameras support are 1 sec, ½ sec, ¼ sec, 1/8th sec, 1/15th sec, 1/30th sec, 1/60th sec, 1/90th sec, 1/125th sec, 1/250th sec, 1/500th sec and 1/1000th sec.

B (Bulb) Setting
The B-setting allows you to manually determine the length of exposure. The shutter will remain open for as long as you keep the shutter release button depressed.

As focal length increases on your lens you will find that you will need to increase the shutter speed in order to reduce the effects of camera shake.

The aperture/shutter speed trade-off
For each aperture setting (f-number) there will be an associated shutter speed that will give you a correctly exposed photograph. Choosing which combination of aperture and shutter speed depends on the type of photo you are taking. For example, for a landscape you will probably want the entire scene in focus, in which you would want a small aperture (high f-number) to achieve a large depth of field. In a wildlife shot however you will probably want a high shutter speed to freeze any motion and also have a small depth of field by using a large aperture to put the background out of focus.

There are many situations where the photographer wants both good depth of field and also a high shutter speed to freeze movement. Often the conditions do not allow this, especially if you are using a telephoto lens. The general rule is that as depth of field increases (narrow aperture) then shutter speed reduces. The photographer must choose which is more important: depth of field or a faster shutter speed, or some in-between compromise.

One compromise is to use a faster film (see the next section on *Film Speed* on page 32), which will allow you to use a higher shutter speed with a good depth of field. However, as will be explained, a fast film produces a grainy effect.

Shutter priority
Shutter priority is a mode that allows you to set the appropriate shutter speed whilst the camera automatically sets the corresponding aperture for the correct exposure. As you change the shutter speed, the aperture will adjust accordingly.

Aperture priority
Aperture priority is a mode that allows you to set the appropriate aperture whilst the camera automatically sets the corresponding shutter speed for the correct exposure. As you change the aperture, the shutter speed will adjust accordingly.

ISO Film speed

- Film/digital sensor speed, expressed as an ISO rating, gives an indication of the sensitivity of the film to light. It applies to both camera roll film and the digital sensors in digital SLR cameras.

- A film with a low ISO rating e.g. ISO 25 is very fine-grained and produces sharp images. It is not very sensitive to light and should be used in bright conditions. It is known as **slow film**.

- A film with an ISO rating 100 to 200 is **medium film.** This should be used in ordinary daylight or indoors.

- A film with a high ISO rating e.g. ISO 1000 is coarse-grained and produces less sharp images. It is very sensitive to light and is useful in low light conditions or where a low shutter speed must be used. It is known as **fast film**.

- ISO stands for **International Standards Organisation**. Another term used for film speed is ASA (American Standards Association). ASA 100 is the same as ISO 100 and so on. ASA is being phased out and replaced by ISO.

- In digital SLR cameras, the digital photocells have a certain sensitivity to light (like film speed) and need to receive just the right amount of light to form a correctly exposed image. Digital photocells also have an ISO rating equivalent to that of traditional roll film. Unlike roll film in which the same ISO rating applies to the *whole* film, digital SLRs allow you to change the ISO rating for *each* photograph you take.

- Typical film speeds are ISO 100, 200 and 400. ISO 400 is twice as sensitive to light as one rated at ISO 200 and needs only half the light to produce a correctly exposed frame of film. ISO 200 is twice as sensitive as ISO 100 and so on.

Exposure

Every subject that we photograph has a certain amount of reflected light. It is this light that determines the subject's brightness. Your SLR has a built-in light meter that uses **Through-The-Lens metering** (TTL-metering) which measures the light entering the lens. The meter calculates the exposure settings required for the particular subject.

We saw earlier how a correctly exposed photograph depends on the shutter speed and aperture. Another factor in the exposure equation is film speed. The **exposure value** can be achieved by altering three elements: the aperture, the shutter speed and the film/digital sensor speed (ISO). Aperture is related to how much light enters the camera. Shutter speed determines for how long the film/sensor is exposed to light and film/sensor speed is a measure of how sensitive the film or sensor is to light. It is defined as an ISO value. Aperture, shutter speed and film/sensor speed are all interrelated. By altering one of these variables, one of the other two will need to be changed by the same amount in order for the exposure to be kept the same.

For example if you have a correctly exposed image with aperture at f/5.6, shutter speed at 1/250th second and a ISO of 200, then if you change the shutter speed say to 1/125th second then you would need to adjust the aperture or ISO by '1 stop' to achieve a correctly-exposed photograph. Since changing the shutter speed from $1/250^{th}$ to $1/125^{th}$ second you are letting in more light (the shutter speed is slower), you would need to change the aperture so that it lets in less light i.e. increase its f-number to f/8. Alternatively you could have changed the ISO to the next value, to one that is less sensitive to light i.e. ISO 100.

Automatic exposure
This refers to the cameras ability to choose the appropriate shutter speed and aperture for the photograph (for a given film speed). It applies in shutter priority mode, aperture priority mode and in programmed modes (the camera makes all the exposure decisions).

Pre-programmed mode settings
Many SLR cameras have special pre-programmed exposure settings for situations such as landscapes, portraits and action photographs. For example, in the landscape mode the camera will choose a small aperture for maximum depth of field, in portrait mode it will select a wide aperture for minimum depth of field and in the action mode it will select the fastest possible shutter speed to freeze the motion.

Manual exposure
Manual exposure is a setting on your camera which allows you to set the aperture and shutter speed manually yourself.

Exposure 'stops'

Exposure stops refer to the changes in values of aperture, shutter speed and ISO (film/sensor speed).

Each time you change from one aperture, shutter speed or ISO number to a neighbouring value then you are changing the exposure by '1 stop'. For example, changing the aperture from f/4 to f/5.6 is 1 stop. Changing the shutter speed from 1/60th second to 1/30th second is 1 stop. Changing the film/sensor speed from ISO 400 to ISO 200 is '1 stop'.

Similarly '2 stops' would be achieved by changing one of these variables by 2 values up or down, for example, changing the ISO from 100 to 400.

Exposure compensation

The light meter in your camera tends to determine exposure based on a mid-tone colour. If however you are photographing a predominantly white or predominantly black scene then the camera will average out the reflected light and produce a grey looking scene. In these cases you will need to adjust the camera manually to produce the effect required. In the case of a white scene you will need to overexpose by +2 stops. You would change one of the variables (aperture, shutter speed or ISO) leaving the other two variables *unchanged*.

This is known as exposure compensation.

Sometimes it is hard for the camera to know the best exposure for a particular situation. In this case you can take the same photograph at a number of different exposure stops to ensure that they have the correctly exposed photograph within the set. This is known as **bracketing**. The three photographs show the effects of bracketing through over and under exposure and how a correctly exposed photograph appears in comparison.

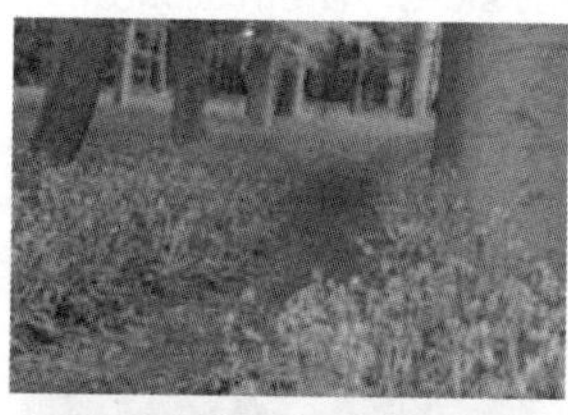

Correctly-exposed

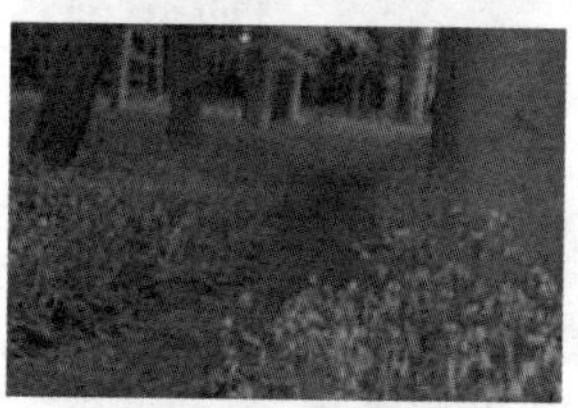

Under-exposed

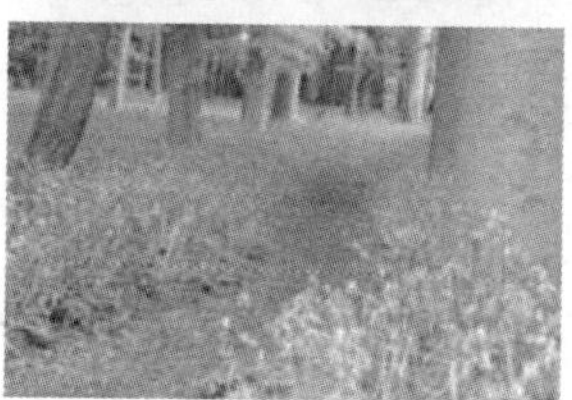

Over-exposed

Digital SLRs: Exposure histograms

Each time you take a photograph with a digital SLR you can view a histogram of the image. The histogram shows the exposure information of the image and you can use it to determine whether your image has been exposed well or not.

The Y-axis of the histogram is the number of pixels and the X-axis is the brightness (from black at the left side to white at the right side). The histogram shows the number of pixels of each colour from black to white.

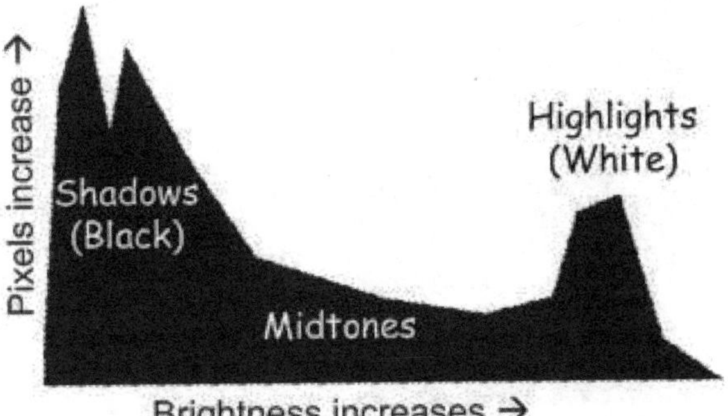

Horizontally it shows the range of colours in your image. The vertical height shows how much of each colour is present.

You should look at the histogram of your photographs to check that you have exposed correctly.

Correct exposure
Correct exposure occurs when the right amount of light reaches the film producing an image that is pleasing to the eye.

A correctly exposed image should have a histogram that neither climbs up at the left or right, but has pixels covering the entire range of the histogram as shown below. A 'bell' shape is the best shape to achieve.

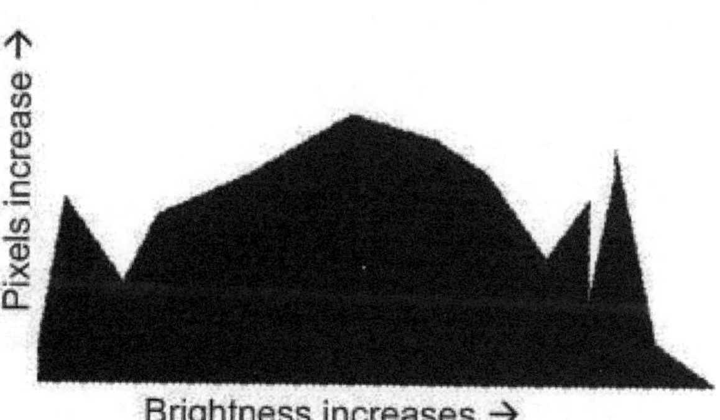

Overexposure
Overexposure occurs when too much light reaches the film producing a lightened print.

A histogram displays an overexposed image with more pixels on the right hand side of histogram, generally climbing up to one or more peaks, as shown below.

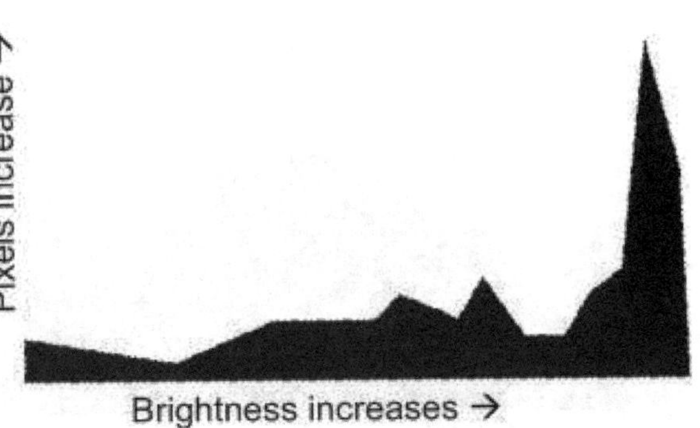

Underexposure
Underexposure occurs when too little light reaches the film, causing a darkened print.

A histogram displays an underexposed image with more pixels on the left hand side of histogram, generally climbing up to one or more peaks, as shown below.

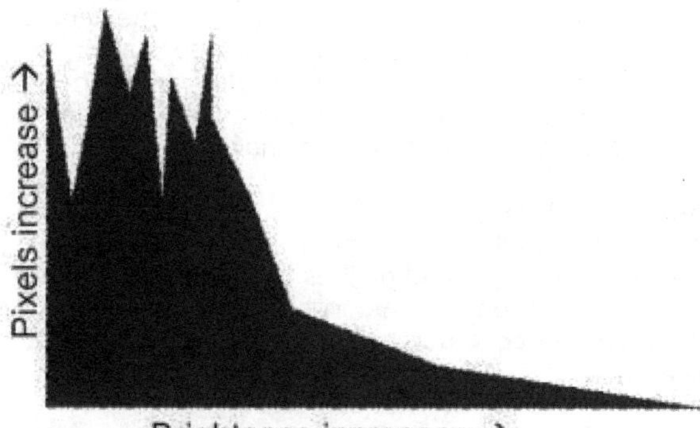

Exposure metering

Exposure Metering
SLR cameras employ a number of exposure metering functions, which determine how your camera measures the light and hence the exposure for a particular shot. There are different metering systems that can be selected for different situations. Some systems just measure the light at the centre of the frame. Others have sophisticated matrix models that measure over the whole frame. The exposure mode you choose is dependant on the type of photograph you are taking:

Matrix Metering
Also called multi-pattern metering or evaluative metering, this method divides the finder image into regions and then uses algorithms in the camera microcomputer to determine the correct exposure. Use this for landscapes. This is usually the default metering system on SLR cameras.

Centre-Weighted Metering
In centre-weighted metering the light is measured primarily (75%) in the centre of the frame, but also measures the light within the entire frame. This is appropriate in instances where there is a main subject in the centre of the frame, such as in portraits. This is still the kind of metering employed on older cameras.

Spot Metering

Spot metering (or partial metering) measures the light only in the centre of the frame. This setting provides very accurate meter readings for small specific areas. It is suitable for images with high contrast content, such as in creating silhouettes.

Auto-Exposure lock

Auto-Exposure lock (AE lock) allows you to take a meter reading from a specific part of an image then hold that reading whilst the image is recomposed. On some cameras the exposure reading can be saved and used over a number of photographs.

Lighting

As we have seen, lighting is very important in determining the exposure required for a photograph. It can also make or break a photograph. Use natural light where possible – such as near a window. If no natural light is available then use a flash or another light source.
Generally if you want to light up the whole of a subject on a photograph, then you must eliminate shadows caused by light sources. Use a reflective surface (see page 70) on the opposite side of a light source to bounce the light back onto the subject.
You also want your lighting to be soft, in which case diffusers can be helpful (see page 71)
In situations where there is a great deal of lighting contrast and the camera is struggling to get the correct exposure, then move up to your subject and take a meter reading just in front of it. Move back to the position where you want to take the picture and shoot at this meter reading (or use spot metering). Don't worry if this is not what the camera suggests – it is being fooled by the contrasts in light.
If you have a digital SLR then you can adjust how the camera responds to light via the white balance functions. For a film SLR you may have to use filters, such as a blue filter when in the presence of tungsten bulb lighting.

Lighting terms

Ambient light
Ambient light is the light surrounding and available to, a subject. It does not include any artificial light supplied by the photographer.

Backlighting
Backlighting is the effect of light, from behind a subject towards the camera. It makes the subject stand out against its background. It can be used to produce a silhouette effect.

Bounce lighting
Bounce lighting is the effect of light (from a tungsten bulb or flash) that is bounced off a reflective surface (see page 70), giving the effect of natural light.

Fill-in light
Fill-in light is additional light from a lamp or flash, used in conjunction with a main light, to help fill in shadows or dark areas that the main light produces. When achieved using a flash, it is called 'fill-in flash'.

Diffuse lighting
Diffuse lighting is low contrast lighting, such as that produced on an overcast day, or by using a diffuser (see page 71). Also known as 'soft lighting'.

Side lighting
Side lighting is the effect of light that hits the object from one side relative to the camera position. It creates shadows and highlights on the subject.

Tungsten and fluorescent light
Tungsten light is light from normal room lamps and ceiling fittings. A blue filter would be applied to your camera to reduce the orange cast caused by this type of lighting. This does not include fluorescent lighting, which would require a pale magenta or a fluorescent-correction filter. With a digital SLR camera, the white balance facility would be set accordingly to correct the casts.

Rim lighting
Rim lighting is created when the main body of object is in silhouette whilst the colour and detail of the object's edges are revealed. Place thick black card between the light and the subject such that only its edges are lit.

Outdoor lighting
Outdoor lighting is at its softest and warmest in the early morning or in the late afternoon or evening. Shadows are long and the light is more even. This is the best time for outdoor photography. In the midday sun the light is at its harshest and can create short shadows and severe lighting contrasts. In these situations it is best to shoot with the sun behind you.

Types of film

- Prior to the introduction of the digital SLR, all SLR cameras were built to use roll film.
- Roll film is a transparent base, coated with a photographic emulsion that can record images.
- There are two types of film: negative film and transparency (or slide) film. It can be colour or black and white.
- Film emulsion is very sensitive to heat, so be careful not to leave your film near a radiator or in a car on a hot day.
- Films come in many sizes such as 120mm or 35mm. SLRs typically use 35mm film.
- Roll film also has a specific film speed, expressed as an ISO number, which determines its sensitivity to light (see the section on ISO Film Speed on page 32).

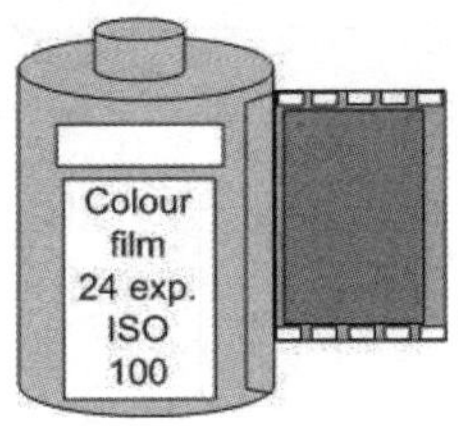

Negative film

- In negative film the colours and tones of a shot are reversed during shooting.
- During film development the process is reversed to produce a 'positive' print. Some of the brightness and quality may be lost in this process.
- Prints can be created from negative film and can be kept as physical photographs to store in an album or to replicate.
- The prints can be copied.
- Negative film is easy to buy and development laboratories are widespread.

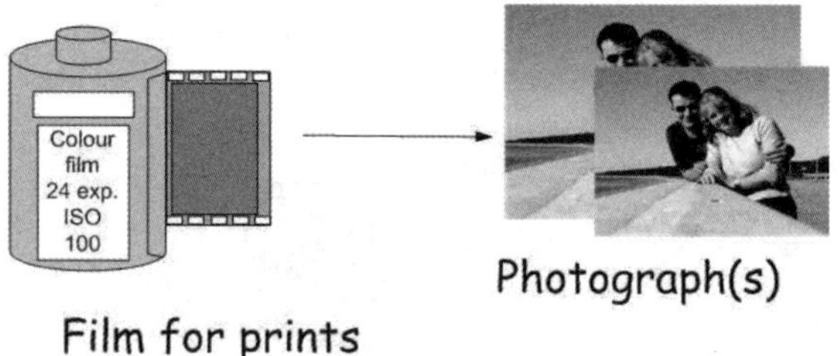

Transparency film

- In transparency (or slide) film the subject is shot as a 'positive'.
- Transparencies give more faithful colour and exposure rendition than negative film since there is no reversal process.
- Transparencies are displayed on a screen via a slide projector.
- Slides cannot be replaced.
- It is more expensive to buy transparency film than negative film, but cheaper to process.
- Preferred medium for publishers as it has a much wider brightness range.

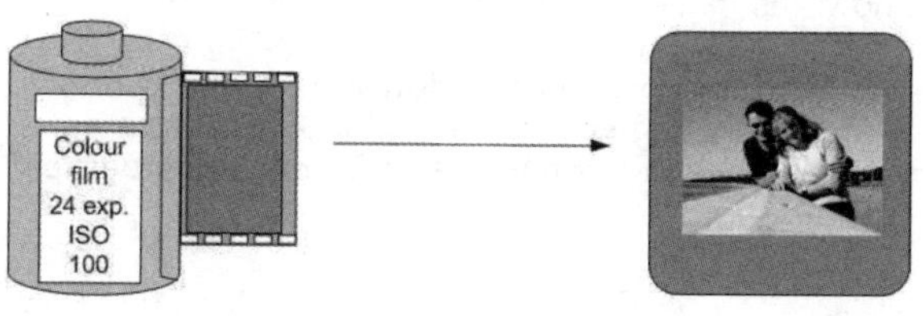

Film for slides

Slide

Uprating/Downrating film

Uprating film
If the film loaded in your camera is too slow for the conditions (for example, the weather worsens and light fades) then you can make your film more sensitive by setting the camera to a higher ISO. For example if you have an ISO 200 film, set your camera to ISO 400. To compensate for this the film development time must be increased by about 30%. This is known as 'pushing' the film.

Downrating film
If the film loaded in your camera is too fast for the conditions (for example, the weather brightens up) then you can make your film less sensitive by setting the camera to a lower ISO. For example if you have an ISO 400 film, set your camera to ISO 200. To compensate for this the film development time must be decreased by about 30%. This is known as 'pulling' the film.

The need for uprating and downrating film is eliminated when you use a digital SLR camera as you can change the film speed for *each* photograph you take.

Digital film

- Digital SLR cameras capture images digitally on an array of light sensitive photocells and so do not require traditional roll film. This allows you to store many more photographs that you could on film and also removes the need to ever change film. The digital memory is reusable. You can delete photographs from it and overwrite with new ones. As a result you can take as many pictures as you want to experiment with new techniques at no extra cost.

- These photocells are held in semiconductor microchips such as **CCD** (Charge-Coupled Device) or **CMOS** (Complementary Metal Oxide Semiconductors) sensors. The sensors react to light by generating an electrical charge. The brighter the light reaching the sensors, the greater the charge generated.

- Image resolution is the amount of detail a digital camera can capture. It is measured in **pixels** (PICture ELements). The more pixels you have the more detail will be recorded and hence the sharper the image will look. This is also known as the **resolution**. It is expressed as either dots per inch or as the height and width of the image in pixels e.g. 1200 x 1800.

- As you increase the number of sensors (photocells) you increase the amount of picture information recorded. A resolution of 6 million pixels is roughly equivalent to that of roll film (to the naked eye).

- Digital film is the storage medium for digital photographs. Also known a **storage cards**, the two most common types are the CompactFlash™ and IBM™ Microdrives. The speed of your storage card refers to how quickly the camera can write the file to the card. Speeds are typically 80x (80 times), 40x, 32x and 16x.

- Once a digital image is captured it is transferred to a storage card. The amount of storage in these mediums is measured in MB (Megabytes) or Gigabytes (GB). Typical storage cards have sizes 128MB, 256MB, 512MB, 1GB, 2GB and 4GB. You should select a card with as large a size as you can afford so that you can store as may images as possible.

- The images can be saved with a level of compression. The lower the compression the greater the image quality. However the image memory size will be large. The higher the compression, the lower the image quality. However, the image memory size will be less, making the storage easier.

Digital SLR cameras

Many of the manufacturers of digital SLR cameras have based their design on their film SLR counterparts. In fact most digital SLRs can be used with lenses designed for film cameras.
The main difference with a digital SLR is the use of a memory card rather than inserting film. The card stores the photographs you take electronically. You are able to delete these photos if you wish or transfer them to a computer or a compact disc. Additionally digital SLRs have a LCD screen on the back of the camera allowing the photographer to view their photograph instantaneously.
There are other differences with digital SLRs, which will be described in the subsequent sections.

If you have recently swapped your film SLR body for a digital SLR body, you may have heard that digital SLR cameras effectively increase the focal length of the lens that you originally used on your film SLR camera (it actually alters the angle of view).
So if you have a 28-70mm zoom lens you effectively get a 42-105mm lens when it is attached to a digital SLR camera. Whilst this may be good news at the top of end of the zoom range, it is not at the wide-angle end, as the 28mm has been replaced with a 42mm lens, which is no longer a wide angle. The reason for this effect is that a digital SLR doesn't actually have a sensor the same size as a 35mm frame - in fact it is a bit smaller. This has the effect of multiplying the focal length of

the lens (by 1.6 times). Full-frame sensors will eliminate this effect giving a 35mm frame - the same as in a film SLR.

Parameter settings
Your digital SLR will have a menu system where you can change various parameters associated with the photograph you are taking. Each manufacturer has approached this differently so you should refer to your manual for the specific details. The most common parameters are:

Image formats: whether you shoot in RAW mode, JPEG (and the quality levels within).

White balance: refers to how your camera responds to certain light conditions such as fluorescent lighting, tungsten bulb lighting, flash daylight and shade.

Colour processing: refers to the hue and saturation that is applied to your images.

Sharpness: how sharp your images are captured on your camera.

ISO film speed: refers to the sensitivity of the photocells in your digital camera to light (like ISO in roll film).

Image formats

Images are stored typically in one of two formats:

- **RAW format**: the image is saved with lossless compression to retain maximum image resolution. Typical image size: 7MB for an image of 1600 x 1200 pixels. RAW mode allows greater control over editing such as correcting for white balance conditions.
- **JPEG format**: the image is a lossy compression format that allows higher compression but still gives good image quality. Most cameras offer Fine and Normal JPEG compression and different resolution levels: Large, Medium and Small.

The best format for quality and manipulation is the RAW format. It allows the greatest flexibility in the conversion stage. Images are converted to **TIFF** (Tagged Image File Format) files via special conversion software. However these take up more storage on your computer (they have lossless compression) and will take longer to load up. With JPEG the storage capacity is much smaller and the time to load and save images is quicker.

RAW mode is the best mode to use for landscapes and wildlife photography where capturing detail is important. JPEG mode is best for action and sports photography where speed of image capture and computer upload/download time is important.

White balance

The white balance functions are designed to correct colour casts caused by various lighting conditions. All colours have a colour temperature measured in degree Kelvins (^{O}K). Red has a low colour temperature and at the other end of the scale, blue has a high temperature. However higher temperature images often appear 'cooler' and lower temperature images appear 'warmer'. Cameras find it hard to adapt to certain lighting conditions, such as fluorescent and tungsten lighting.
With film cameras it is advisable to use a blue filter, for example, to correct the low temperature of tungsten lighting to create a white cast rather than the orange cast that the tungsten light creates. With digital SLR cameras there are parameters that can be set to control how the camera responds to certain lighting, without the need for a filter. This parameter is known as the **white balance**.
Your camera manual will instruct you on your particular white balance functions but, in general, you will set the white balance in accordance to the current lighting situation: daylight, shade, fluorescent lighting, tungsten lighting, flash or the custom white balance.
If you shoot in RAW mode then the white balance setting will not affect the photograph – it can be adjusted in the computer editing stage.

Colour processing

Colour processing parameters allow you to adjust the hue, saturation and contrast of your images. Most of the time it is best to leave these at their standard values but you may want to increase saturation for certain situations.

Sharpness

The sharpness function determines the level of sharpness an image will have when you download it to your camera. An image that has been sharpened in the camera will suffer if further image processing is required. An image that is unsharpened in the camera will be more adaptable to manipulation after download to the computer.

Professionals always set the sharpening to its minimum level, whether you are shooting in RAW or JPG. The image can be sharpened once it has been downloaded.

ISO film speed (see page 32)

You can change the sensitivity to light of the digital sensor by altering the ISO value. Digital SLRs allow you to change the ISO rating for *each* photograph you take.

EXIF

The Exchangeable Image File (EXIF) format is the data about a photograph that is stored along side the image on the digital camera's memory card. This data includes the date and time the photograph was taken and what settings the photograph was taken at such as shutter speed, ISO, aperture, white balance, focal length, file size, and metering mode.
The sample of typical EXIF data for a photograph is shown here.

```
File Name
        IMG0001.JPG

Camera Model Name
        Canon EOS 300D DIGITAL

Shooting Date/Time
        01/12/2004 14:35:25

Shooting Mode
        Program AE

TV(Shutter Speed)
        1/125

Av(Aperture Value)
        7.1

Metering Mode
        Evaluative

Exposure Compensation
        0
```

ISO Speed
100

Lens
28.0 - 200.0 mm

Focal Length
32.0 mm

Image Size
3072x2048

Image Quality
Fine

Flash
Off

White Balance
Shade

AF Mode
AI Focus AF

Parameters
Contrast Normal
Sharpness Normal
Colour saturation Normal
Colour tone Normal

Colour Space
Adobe RGB

File Size
5814KB

The Digital Darkroom

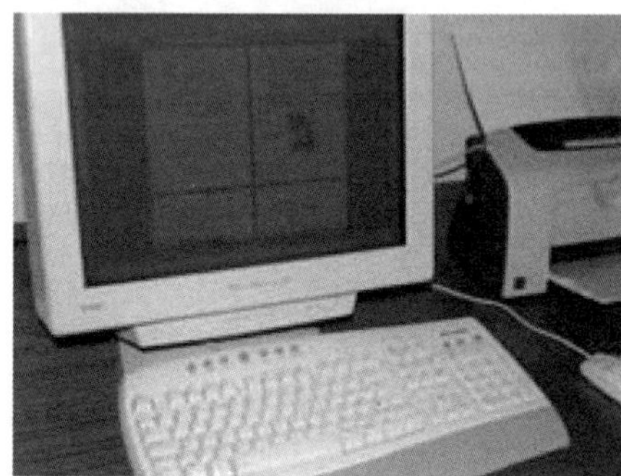

The digital darkroom refers to the computer equipment needed to take your digital images from your camera, edit or manipulate those images, then, if you require a physical print, to print them out on photographic paper.

Downloading your photographs from your camera memory card to your computer or printer can done via cable (e.g. USB). Some printers allow direct download from the memory card. Alternatively you can download your images into a portable device.

If you are using a film SLR camera then you have the option of scanning your negatives or prints with a scanner connected to your computer.

Once you have your images stored on your computer you can then use one of the many images manipulation software packages to perform various manipulations, such as cropping, enlarging, editing parts of the image, applying a filter, sharpening, adjusting brightness and contrast, to name just a few.

It is very important that you have a computer that has adequate RAM (Random Access Memory) for storing the image data temporarily whilst you edit it. Additionally you must have lots of storage memory (hard disk space) - in the region of 100GB+ to store your images permanently.

Finally once you have edited your image, you may want to print it out on photographic paper. It is important to have a printer that is designed for photographic images i.e. with high resolution e.g. 2800x1400 dpi. Those printers with separate cartridges for each colour are the best - especially for printing skin tones.

Colour management
You may have noticed already that the photograph you see on your digital SLR LCD screen to that on your computer monitor and that printed on paper out are never the same in terms of colour. Each device interprets colour in its own way and you must calibrate them appropriately so these differences are kept to a minimum.
There are some standard colour profiles (also known as International Colour Convention (ICC) profiles) that you can set your devices to. There are two that have been adopted by digital SLR manufacturers: Adobe 1998 and sRGB. If you stick to one profile and set your camera, PC, editing software and printer profile to this then this will minimise the differences between the colour interpretations on the different devices.

Storage on your computer
With film cameras you probably stored your photographs in albums. With digital cameras you still have the ability to print out your photographs and store them in this manner. However you may want to store your images on your computer and view them via your monitor. This will save on paper and ink costs and if you buy the appropriate software you can organise your photographs into categories, give descriptions to each photo and have the ability to put on slide shows on your monitor.

It is important however that you back-up your photographs onto an external storage such as CD-ROM or even better a DVD writer so you have a second copy if something disastrous happens, such as a hard disk crash.

Portable storage
If you are away from home you may take more photographs than can be stored on your memory card. In this case you may want to invest in a separate portable storage device to download your photographs to, after which you can delete from your camera's memory card and take another set. This is especially important if shooting in RAW mode where the size of images is large.

Summary

This page will summarise what has been described in this section by listing the main things that you should think about when taking a photograph. There are a number of questions you should ask yourself:

What do I want in focus?

Consider the depth of field – do I want everything in focus (large depth of field) or just one particular item and the rest blurred (small depth of field)? You need to select the appropriate aperture and focal length. You will also need to consider how far you are from your subject, as this will affect the depth of field.

How much do I want in the photo?

Do you want a wide view, such as in a landscape, or do I want to zoom in to one particular feature? You need to choose the appropriate lens and focal length.

Is my subject moving and if so, do I want it in sharp focus?

You will need to consider the shutter speed to freeze the motion and possibly use a tripod if the conditions allow it.

What are the lighting conditions like?

If the light is poor you may need to select a faster film speed, use a flash, select a white balance or select a slower shutter speed. If the light is good then you may need to use reflectors or diffusers to soften it, attach a filter, use a lens hood to reduce glare or take advantage of a higher shutter speed.

SLR Camera Accessories

Types of lenses

Standard lens
A standard lens has a focal length of 50mm. It records perspective in much the same way that the human eye sees it.

Prime lens
A prime lens is a lens that has a fixed focal length e.g. 35mm lens.

Wide-angle lens
A wide-angle lens provides an extensive depth of field at small apertures and wide angle of view. It has a short focal length e.g. 17mm. They are most commonly used in landscape photography.

Telephoto lens
A telephoto lens makes subjects appear larger on the film than a normal lens would at the same distance from the subject. Telephoto lens refer to those lenses with a focal length of 300mm or greater and hence they have a narrower angle of view. They also have a shallow depth of field. They are often used in wildlife photography.

Zoom lens
A zoom lens is a lens that allows you to adjust the focal length over a range of focal lengths e.g. 35mm-80mm.

Long focus lens
A long focus lens has a focal length greater than 50mm.

Macro lens (Close-up lens)
A macro lens is specially designed to allow you to focus on close-up subjects and can achieve reproduction ratios of subjects in the region of 1:2 or even 1:1 (life–size).

Fish-eye lens
A fish-eye lens has a focal length of 15mm and has 180 degrees angle of vision.

Mirror lens
The advantage of a mirror lens is that it provides magnification yet the lens itself is short in length. It does this through a concave primary mirror and a convex secondary mirror, which reflect light back and forth thus creating a long focal length. It has a fixed aperture, usually small, that can be restrictive, as it cannot provide any real depth of field.
Hence it is good for creating close-ups of distant objects.
The mirror lens is often used in special effects as it produces 'doughnuts' – out-of-focus rings that can be used to good effect.

Image stabilisation lens

Photographs can be ruined by camera shake. Image stabilisation lenses correct any movement caused by camera shake by freezing the subject at exposure. They are useful for close-ups or when a slow shutter speed is required. As a result they are priced at the top end of the market. Most image stabilisation lenses are zoom lenses.

Tilt and shift lens

Tilt and shift (TS) lenses provide additional flexibility to your photography.

With a normal lens it can be difficult to get the depth of field on a subject that is at an angle to the camera. Using the **tilt** movements on a TS lens moves the plane of focus so that a subject can appear totally sharp along its whole length.

The **shift** movements of the lens aid in the photography of tall objects, such as buildings. With a normal lens, as you point the camera upwards, the plane of the camera film is no longer parallel to the plane of the object and as a result the object will appear to be 'falling over' also known as 'convergence'. Having the shift movements in a TS lens you will not have to tilt the lens up to include the top of the subject.

Tripod & camera supports

- Ideally you should support your camera for all shots. A tripod is the obvious piece of equipment, but you can always improvise with placing the camera on a table, window ledge etc. This is particularly useful when using slow shutter speeds or a telephoto lens or other situations when camera-shake would be noticeable.

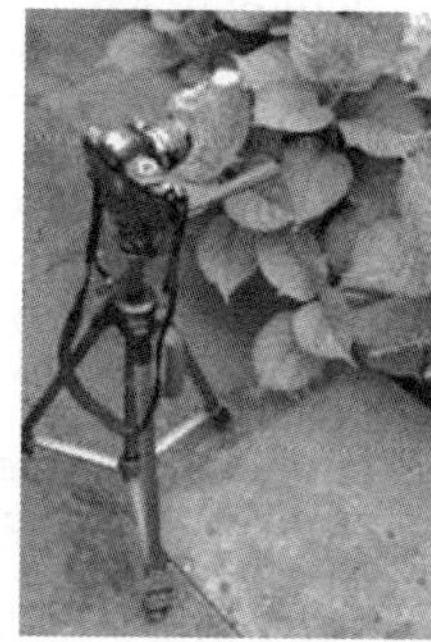

- A **tripod** is a three-legged structure on which your camera can be mounted. There are also **unipods** (one leg). In some situations where there is limited space or you don't have time to assemble a tripod, a unipod, having a single leg, can be set up quickly and fit into the tightest of spaces. They are also much lighter to carry.

- There are other camera supports, such as a clamp type that can be attached to the edge of table. Small **beanbags** are also useful for keeping your camera steady on uneven surfaces.

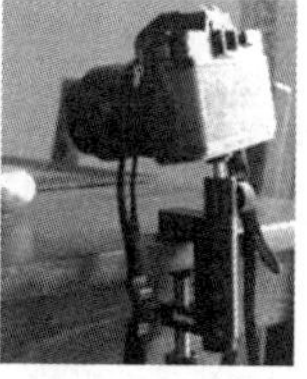

Reflectors & Diffusers

- Reflectors can be anything that reflects light onto a subject. You can use card, a Lastrolite folding reflector, a silver umbrella reflector or a natural reflector.

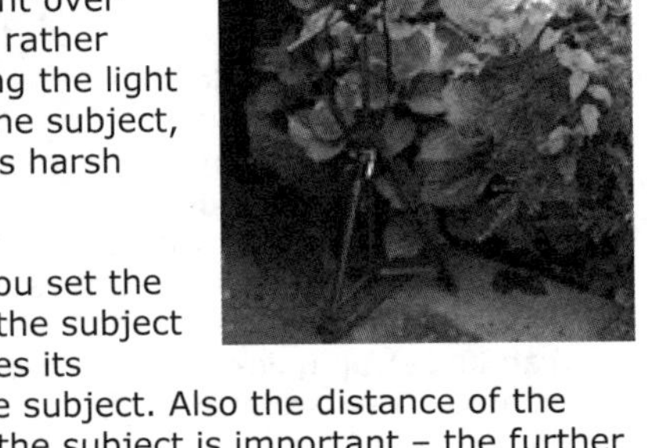

- Reflectors help to eliminate shadows in photographs. When used in conjunction with a flash, they bounce a light over the subject, rather than directing the light straight at the subject, which causes harsh shadows.

- The angle you set the reflector to the subject at determines its effect on the subject. Also the distance of the reflector to the subject is important – the further the reflector, the weaker the effect.

- In this photograph a large sheet of artist's card is being used with a flash unit, that's titled towards it, to reflect the light over the flowers. A diffuser could be used in the same way.

White reflectors
White reflectors are useful for creating a softer light effect such as in portraits. If you are on a budget, use white card but use it close to the subject, as it is not an efficient reflector.

Silver reflectors
Silver reflectors are more efficient than white reflectors and must be held further away. They are often used in the form of umbrellas, seen in many professional studios. Use with caution as they can produce harsh light and cause people to squint. If you are on a budget, scrunch up aluminium foil and attach to card.

Gold reflectors
Use gold reflectors to warm up the light it reflects.

Black reflectors
Black reflectors *reduce* reflections on the subject. Fashion photographers will use them for highlighting cheekbones and facial contours of a model's face.

Diffusers
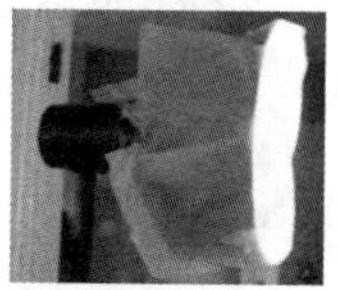
Diffusers come in many forms – as covers for light sources (see photograph) or as panels that are held near the subject to direct a diffused light onto the subject. They have the effect of light on an overcast day and spread the light evenly over the subject.

Filters

- A filter is a coloured piece of glass or other transparent material that is placed over the lens to produce effects, such as to highlight or eliminate a colour or to produce an artistic effect.

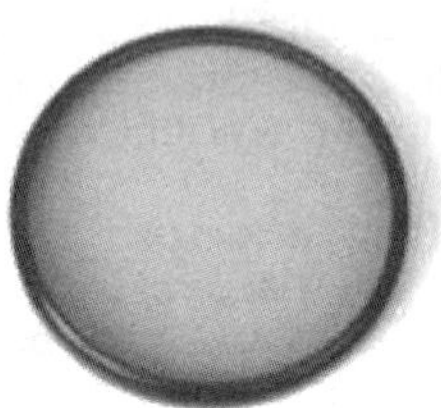

- You can use more than one filter at a time. However the more filters you use, the more you lose in sharpness in the final photograph.

  There are two types of filter:

  - Round filters that screw directly onto the front of the lens (screw-in filters).

  - Square filters that slot into a filter holder, which is attached to the front of the lens. You can fit more than one filter in the holder at a time.

- Filters must be handled at the edges and stored away when not in use so that they are kept free from dust and scratches.

Polarising filter

If you buy only *one* filter, buy a polarising filter. A polarising filter blocks out light (polarises the light passing through it) and so

- Colour saturation is increased. Blue skies, for example, appear much deeper in colour.
- Reduces glare on non-metallic surfaces, such as foliage.
- Reduces or eliminates reflections in surfaces such as glass, water and metal. However you must make sure you are not at 90 degrees to the reflected surface - best is at about 30 degrees.

When using a polarising filter outdoors for the deepening of colours, it is best to have the sun perpendicular to the camera axis i.e. at your side. It is very useful on dull and overcast days to cut through the glare that can appear on wet foliage.

The best type of polarising filter is the circular filter, which attaches to the front of the lens. You can rotate the filter to achieve the effect you require. At a certain rotation the polarising effect will be at its maximum (reflections will be minimised).

UV filter

A UV filter filters out UV light to eliminate blue hazes.

Use a UV filter or a protector filter to prevent damage to your lens. A dirty or scratched lens can cause light dispersion or flare.

Leave it on your lens permanently. A filter is much cheaper to replace than a new lens!

Colour filters

The camera does not interpret certain lighting conditions the same way as the human eye does. Colour filters are really known as colour balancing filters as they are intended to help record a coloured scene in the same way that the eye sees it.

There are three types of colour filters:

- Colour correction
- Colour conversion
- Colour compensation

Correction filters

- Colour correction filters balance slight changes in the colour of light. Examples: the '81' series of warm-up filters and the '82' series of cool blue filters.

- Warm-up filters are similar to orange filters but subtler. They are effective in 'warming-up' views, neutralising blue casts found in skies and in portraits, to give skin a healthy glow. Filter codes are 81A (weakest), 81B & 81C (strongest).

- Cool blue filters remove excess warmth from light. They are useful in foggy weather to give a bluer tint.

Conversion filters

- Colour conversion filters are stronger versions of correction filters and come in two series: the blue '80' series and the orange '85' series.
- The blue '80' series remove orange casts, especially those caused by tungsten lighting. They are also useful for giving a scene a blue cast.
- The orange '85' series balance any strong blue casts found in light.
- Digital SLRs remove the need for conversion filters as they have a white balance control that lets you alter the setup for indoor photography.

Compensation filters

- Colour compensation filters balance the colour casts created from other light sources, such as fluorescent light bulbs and sodium vapour.
- They are not as common as the other types of colour filters but are often used by professional interior photographers.
- An example is the pale magenta filter, which is used to reduce the cast from fluorescent lighting.

Colour filters

Pure colour filters are used in black and white photography, but can be used in colour photography if a special effect is desired.

Yellow filter
A yellow filter adds contrast to clouds, lightens up skin, freckles and blonde hair.

Orange filter
An orange filter darkens sky tones and brings out the texture of stone buildings.

Green filter
A green filter darkens skins and lips.

Red filter
A red filter helps to create dramatic dark skies.

Blue filter
A blue filter darkens skies. Also prevents indoor photographs having strong yellow/orange casts from standard (tungsten) room lighting.

Sepia filter
A sepia filter gives that 'old-time' brown look.

Other Filters

Neutral density filter
A neutral density filter reduces the amount of light that reaches the film. Use in bright conditions to reduce the light intensity.

Soft-focus filter
A soft-focus filter is used for softening up subjects such as skin. Gives that dreamy look. Good for wedding photographs, for example. Use with slight over-exposure (+½ or +1 stops) for a stronger effect.

Graduate filter
A graduate filter is part coloured, part clear. Used to affect the sky in the top half of a picture, for example, leaving the bottom half of the picture unaffected.

Skylight filter
A skylight filter filters out UV light but has a slight pink tinge to it – 'warms up' an outdoor photograph on sunny days.

Close-up filter
A close-up filter allows photographs to be taken at a distance closer than the lens would normally allow, thus magnifying subjects.

Diffuser filter
A diffuser filter diffuses the light to create a soft effect, eliminating harsh lighting.

Centre spot filter
A centre spot filter keeps the central part of the photograph clear but diffuses the surroundings.

Diffractor filter
A diffractor filter diffracts the light into a spectrum of colour.

Star filter
A star filter creates twinkling stars from lights. Also known as a 'star-burst' filter.

Vignetting
Vignetting is the darkening of the corners around an image, slide or print. It can be due to many things such as a lens hood being too small, poor lens quality or to filters not being large enough. Using more than one filter can also cause this effect.
In the photograph, the filter has caused darkening of the top corners.

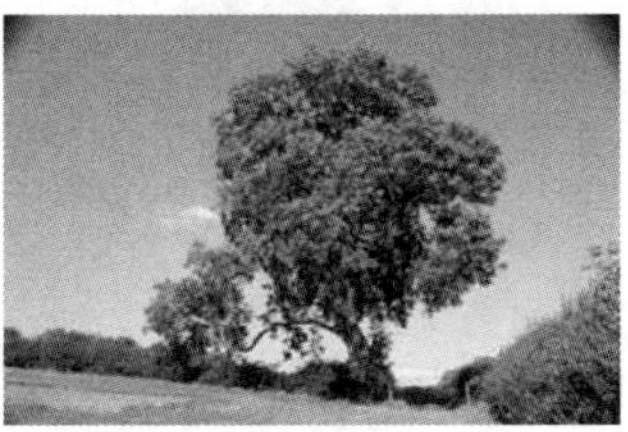

Extension tubes

- Extension tubes are rings placed between the camera and the lens. They are not lenses themselves.

- They are used for close-up macro photography.

- They simply extend the distance between the lens and the camera, thus magnifying subjects. They are available in many sizes and you can use them separately or combine them to produce the effect you require.

- They must be used close-up to the subject. Use a tripod!

- They can be bought fairly cheaply (compared to the cost of lenses).

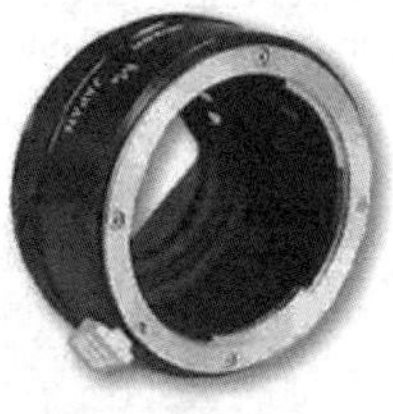

Flash

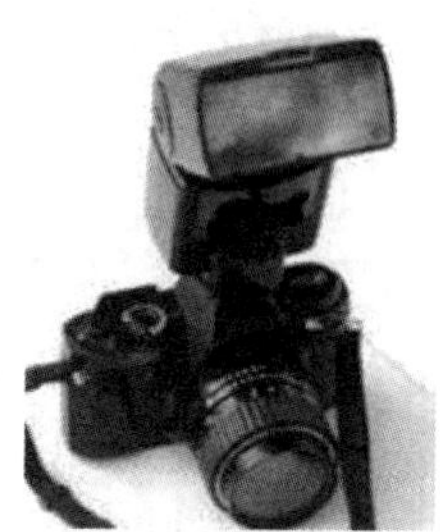

- A flash is a short, intense burst of light from a light bulb or an electronic flash unit. It is used when there is insufficient ambient light available for a particular scene.

- Some flash units are built into the camera. Alternatively you can buy a separate flash unit (flashgun) to mount on the hot-shoe. These will provide much more light than the built-in flash. A unit with a swivel head is best as these can be directed towards reflected surfaces, rather than directly at the subject (which can create harsh shadows). A *dedicated* flashgun when attached to your camera will take detail from your camera to ensure that the correct level of flash is delivered.

- A flashgun has a flash-sync speed which is the maximum shutter speed that can be used with the flash. Often this is $1/125^{th}$ second. You can select this shutter speed or one below this.

- The guide number (GN) of a flash is the measure of its power. The higher the GN, the more power it has. Flash fall-off occurs when your flash is not powerful enough to reach the subject being photographed.

Lens hood

- A lens hood is a collar placed around the front of the lens. It reduces unwanted light flare on the lens when shooting into the sun.

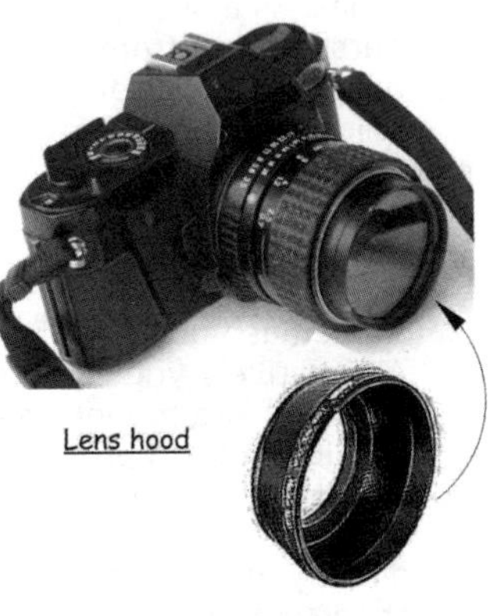

- They are generally circular in shape, though other shapes are available and they can be folding or fixed.
- It must be large enough not to cause vignetting (the darkening of the corners around an image).
- Keeping your lens clean also reduces flare. If you don't have a lens hood, trying using your hand to shade your lens.

Light meters

- A light meter measures the brightness of light and is used to calculate the amount of exposure required for a particular scene. Your camera will have a built-in light meter (using TTL metering) that measures the *reflected* light off a subject. This is adequate for most situations.

- However you can purchase a hand-held incident light meter, which can provide very accurate meter readings by measuring the light *falling* on a subject. The photographer reads the meter close to the subject then sets his camera's aperture and shutter speed accordingly. You may have seen wedding and portrait photographers using this technique.

- Hand-held meters do not take into account any filters that you may have on your camera.

Light box

- A light box is a box containing a light with a translucent surface. The light is usually provided by daylight-balanced fluorescent tubes, which offer an even lighting across the box.

- It is used to view slides and negatives. A **loupe** (a magnifying lens) is often used to view the finer detail of the slides.

- It can also be used in close-up photography for providing backlight to small objects.

Cable release/Remote switch

- A cable release / remote switch is an attachment to your camera that allows you to activate the shutter release button at a distance away from the camera, without you having to touch the button yourself.

- They are particularly useful for eliminating camera shake. Even with your camera on a tripod, pressing the shutter release button can cause camera shake.

- They are also useful in situations when you do not want to be constantly sitting behind your camera waiting for the perfect shot to appear, such as in wildlife photography. You can sit at a safe distance away from the camera and activate the shutter release when necessary.

- The **cable release** is typically a manual contraption attached to your camera that works on air pressure. The pressure applied inside the cable that forces a pin downwards on the shutter release button thus simulating that of a finger pressing the button.

- The **remote switch** works electronically and is plugged into your camera in a specific socket. At the other end of the cable the photographer operates the camera by a small hand-held console. **Wireless remote controls** are also available, doing away with the cable. They must be pointed towards the camera for shutter release.

- The remote switch is much better to use than the manual cable releases. The latter can be quite fiddly to set up and, as it involves the actual depression of the shutter release button, there is always the possibility of camera shake. With the remote switch, the actual shutter release button is never depressed.

Backgrounds

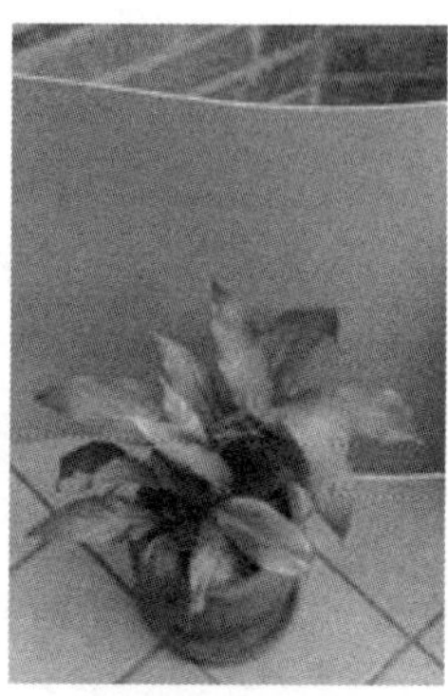

- A background is the scene that appears behind the principal subject of a picture. It can be a natural background, such as sky or foliage. Alternatively you can purchase an artificial background – a large piece of card depicting a pattern, picture or plain colour, as in the photograph here.

- The background should be uncluttered so it does not take any attention away from the main subject.

- Having a background out of focus can help emphasise the main subject. Use a wide aperture for this effect e.g. f/4 or f/5.6.

Photographic Techniques

Rule of Thirds

- The 'Rule of Thirds' suggests that the position of a subject in a photograph can be more 'dramatic' or interesting if placed either one third from the left, or one third up from the bottom.

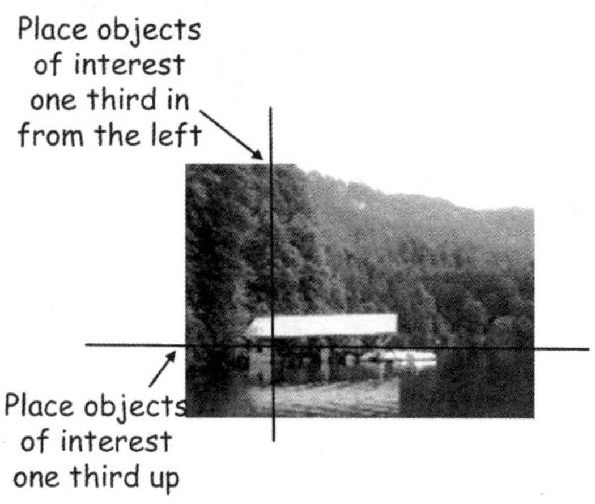

- Can be applied to a variety of assignments, in particular landscapes and skylines.

- Typically applies to landscapes where the skyline is one third of the way up the print, or a tree that is placed on third from the left, for example.

Silhouettes

- You can create silhouettes in your photographs by exposing for the highlighted parts of a scene (such as the sun). This underexposes, and hence silhouettes, the darker parts of the scene.

- For example, a boat on water against a sunset can be silhouetted, by exposing for the lightest part of the sky (using spot metering). The boat will be underexposed and appear as a black shape against the red sunset.

- You may want to use AE lock if your camera supports it. It would allow you to take a meter reading (spot meter) from the highlighted part of the image then hold that reading whilst the image is recomposed. An alternative is to underexpose your image by -2 stops.

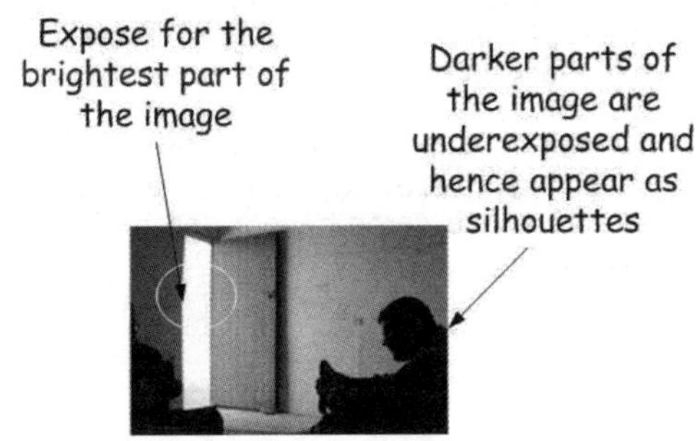

Depth of field

In many photographs it is important to know what is going to be in focus and what isn't. In some cases, such as a landscape, we would want the entire photograph to be in focus (large depth of field). A close-up of a flower however, would require just the flower in focus with the whole of the background out of focus (small depth of field). The choice of lens, aperture and how close we are to the subject are important factors in determining the depth of field:

To create a large depth of field:
- Set a small aperture e.g. f/16.
- Use a small focal length lens e.g. 35mm.
- Keep back from the subject.

To create a small depth of field:
- Set a wide aperture e.g. f/5.6.
- Use a long focal length lens e.g. 200mm.
- Move in close to the subject.

Older cameras have scale markings on them, which can be used to estimate the depth of field. Some modern electronic cameras have a depth of field preview function.

Leading the eye

- To 'lead the eye' in a photograph to a subject, put something in the foreground that leads to that something in the background. It is useful for drawing attention to something in the distance.

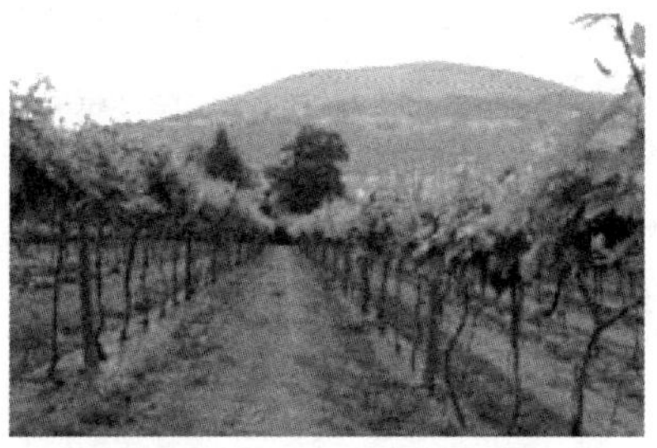

- Use a wide-angle lens.

- Examples are:
A wall that stretches into the distance,
A rope leading from the shore to a boat,
A path leading down a garden or,
as in this photograph, a row of vines stretching down a field.

Bracketing

Bracketing involves taking several different shots of the same subject, each at a different exposure so that you have a range of darker and lighter exposures. It is useful if there is doubt as to which is the best exposure for the photograph. It is likely that the perfectly exposed photograph will be amongst the bracketed photos you have taken.

On most SLR cameras there is a bracketing facility. The bracketing display will look a bit like the display below. In this case -1, 0 and +1 stops have been chosen for the bracketing set.

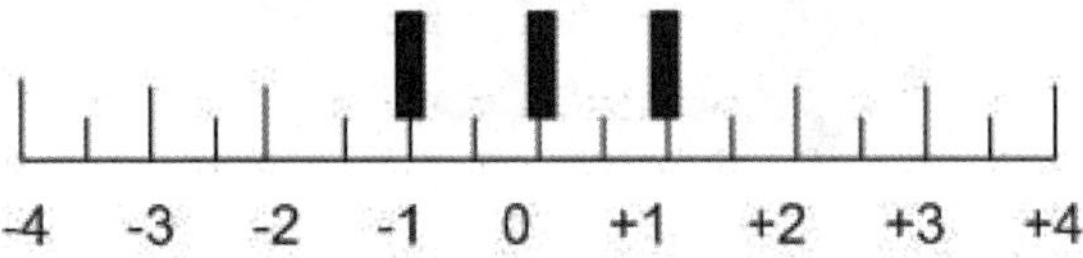

If there is no bracketing facility, then the photographer can manually set consecutive photographs to be exposed at different exposure stops.

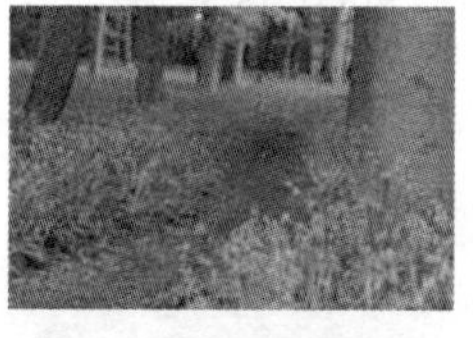

These photographs are of the same scene taken at three different exposures.

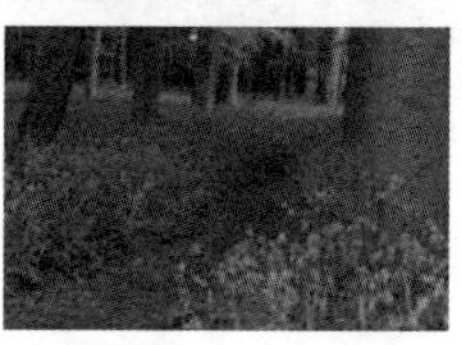

Each photo varies by 1 stop.
The top photo is the best exposed.

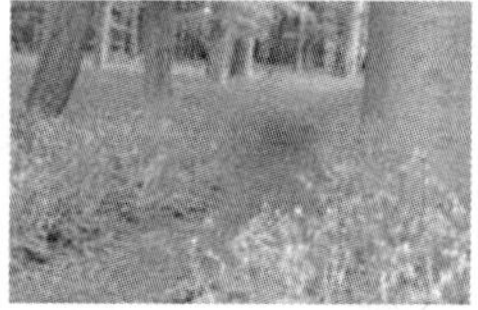

The middle photo is under-exposed and the bottom one is over-exposed.

Mostly-white scenes

- A scene that is mostly white, such as snowy scene or a white cat on a white sheet, can result in a greyish looking photograph since the camera tries to average out the colour.

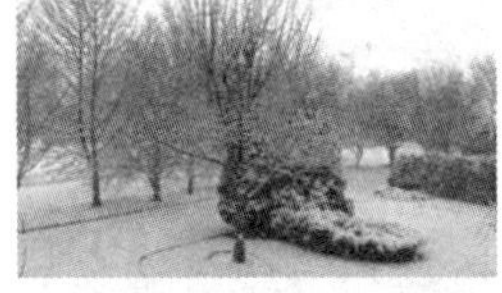

- The camera is fooled into underexposing the shot because the light tones reflect too much light and the camera tries to record them as mid-tones.

- You must over-expose to compensate for this. Try +1 or +2 stops.

Mostly-dark scenes

- A scene that is mostly dark, such as a black cat on a black sheet can result in a greyish looking photograph since the camera tries to average out the colour.

- The camera is fooled into over-exposing the shot because the dark tones reflect too little light and the camera tries to record them as mid-tones.

- You must under-expose to compensate for this. Try –1 or -2 stops.

Light contrasts

- Some shots need to deal with varying intensities in light, such as someone sitting in front of a window on a sunny day. Outside the light is bright; inside it is dull.
- Exposing for the sky outside in this case will put the subject in silhouette.
- Expose for the main subject so that it is correctly exposed.
- Use a filter, such as a diffuser to soften the light.
- If in doubt, use the bracketing facility to obtain several images at different exposures.
- The best time to take outdoor photography is in the early morning or evening when the light is at its softest and shadows are long.

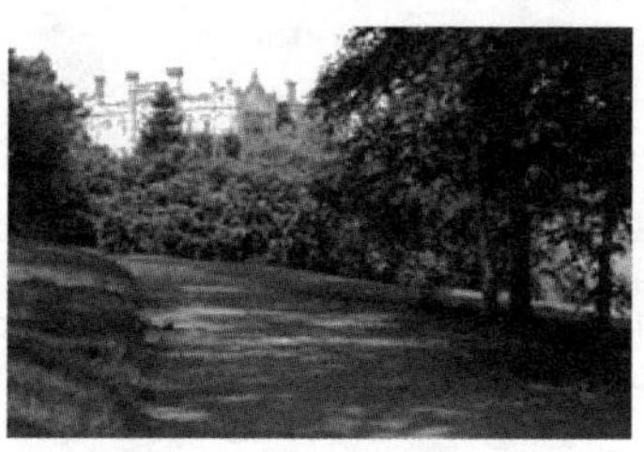

Flash

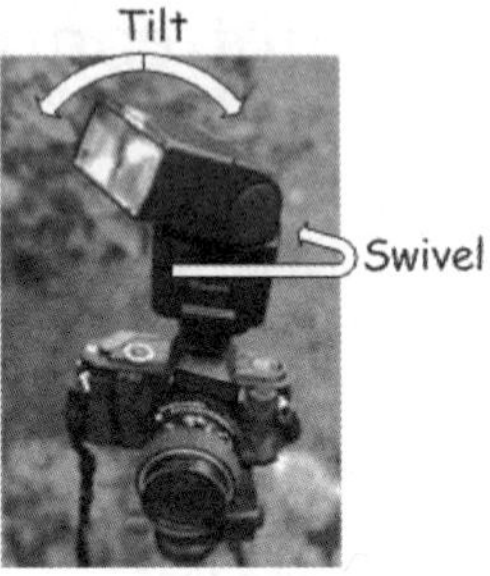

- A flash is useful for creating extra light on a subject. However, pointing it directly at a subject can create some harsh shadows. It is much better to direct the flash at a reflective surface that bounces the light onto the subject. This is particularly important in taking portraits, as flashing directly into people's eyes can cause red-eye. It is a good idea to purchase a flash unit that has a swivel head that can be swivelled and tilted.

- Take care not to shoot the flash onto reflective surfaces such as mirrors. The reflections from these surfaces can be harsh and 'washed-out'. The photo here shows what happens when you shoot into a mirror with a flash.

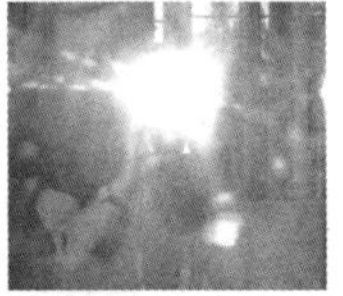

- For portraits, try bouncing the flash off a corner rather than a flat surface for a more diffuse light. Do not bounce your flash off a coloured surface - unless you want your subject to have a coloured cast!

- Flash is particularly useful in close-up and macro photography where the small apertures require long shutter speeds (leading to camera shake).

Red eye

Red-eye is caused by bright light (e.g. a flash) bouncing off the red blood cells behind the retina. Children are the most susceptible to red-eye. It can be reduced by asking to subject to look at a bright light just prior to the flash going off (to constrict their pupils). Some cameras have a red-eye reduction feature that fires a bright light just before the flash goes off.

Fill-in Flash

When the light levels between the main subject and its surroundings are very similar then fill-in flash will help the make the main subject stand out. It is useful in dull weather or in the shade. It can be used outdoors as well as indoors. It is useful when the subject is back-lit, putting the front of the main subject in the shade, or when there is a bright sun putting the main subject in shadow.

It is best not to use too much flash power – only about a half or quarter is necessary. The built-in flash on your camera may be sufficient for this as it has less power than a separate flash unit. Underexposure occurs when your subject is too far away for your flash to have any effect. Each flash has a certain about of power and its specification will tell you its range.

Framing the picture

- This has nothing to do with frames that you put a photograph into and hang on the wall!
- Framing a picture is a natural frame within the photograph, such as tree or a doorway. It creates a natural border around the main subject to help draw the eye to towards it.
- Examples are arches, overhanging tree and man-made structures.
- You can frame beneath the subject as well as above.

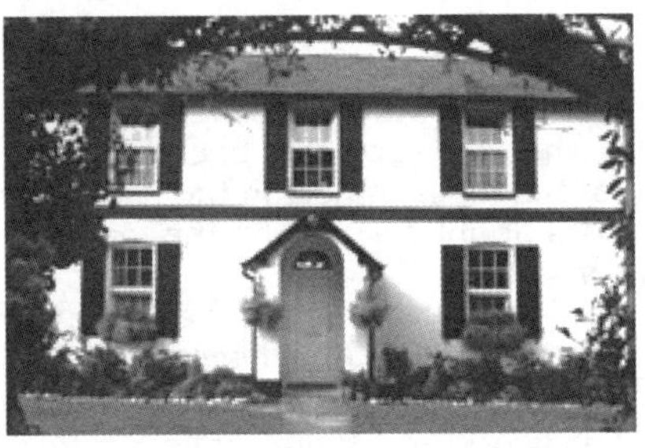

Zoom burst

- Zoom burst effects are created by zooming the lens from one end of its focal length range to the other during an exposure.
- The subject is depicted as an explosion of streaks.

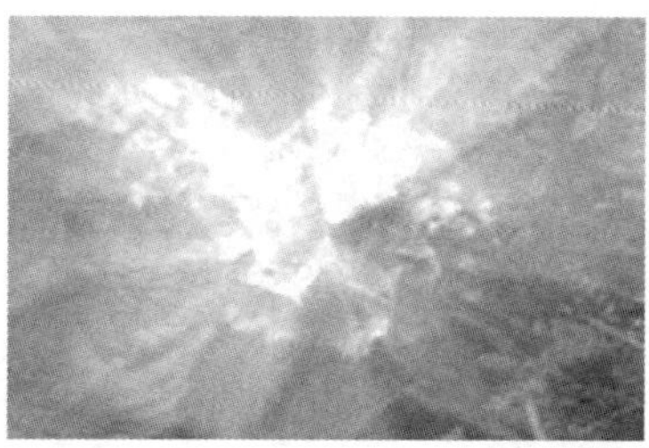

- Use simple, bold subjects.
- It requires a zoom lens. Use a shutter speed of 1 second or more so that you have enough time to zoom through the full range.
- You must use a tripod and be as smooth as possible in twisting the lens through its zoom range. It takes practice!

Deepen colours

- To deepen colour saturation, slightly underexpose (by −½ to −1 stops). It will make colours appear much darker. Try not to underexpose too much. It is especially useful in bright conditions where subjects would normally appear washed-out.

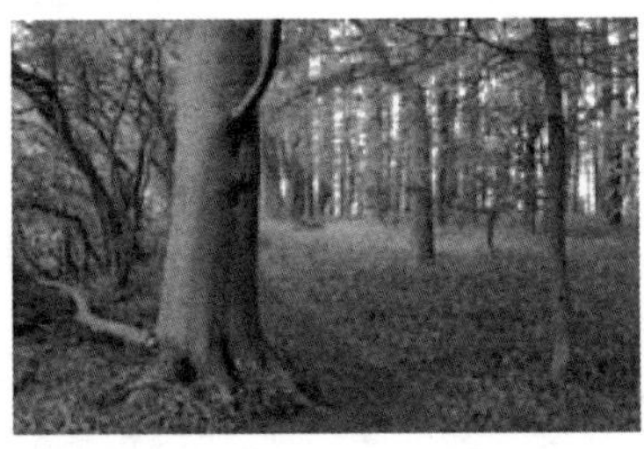

- Alternatively, use a polarising filer for deeper colour saturation.

'Reveal' the subject

- In some photographs the main subject can often be lost amongst other items in the picture or within a cluttered background. There are several techniques to 'bring out' your main subject.

- If you cannot get close to the subject then use a small depth of field so that any background items are put out of focus. It is easier to put the background out of focus if you use a wide aperture and stand as far away as possible from the subject - but use a tripod!

- Move around until you have a simple, uncluttered background.

- For some shots of a particular subject, such as a child, get close to the subject. This has several advantages:

  - It eliminates any background clutter that may distract away from the main subject.

  - It makes it very clear what the photograph is of.

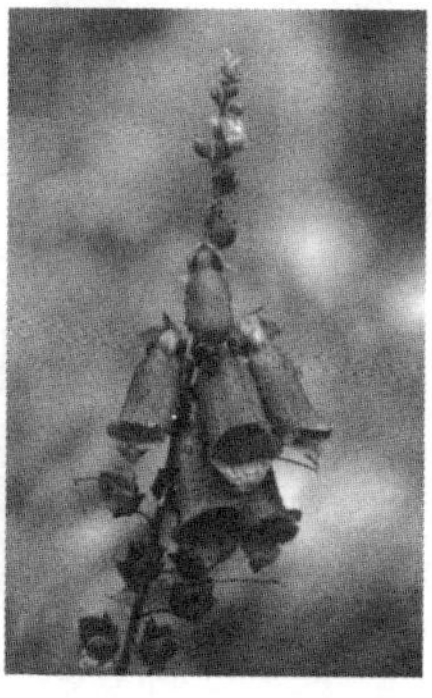

Try different angles

- Don't always go for the standard shot of something, such as a famous landmark.
- Try taking an unusual view - move around your subject - you may find something interesting; such as some foreground detail that brings the photograph to life.
- Don't just stand there! Try crouching down and shooting upwards. Or find a wall or stairs to climb and get a shot looking down on the subject. You can also try to shoot with the camera at waist level. The following photograph was taken crouching down so that the sky and mountains would appear in the background behind the donkey.

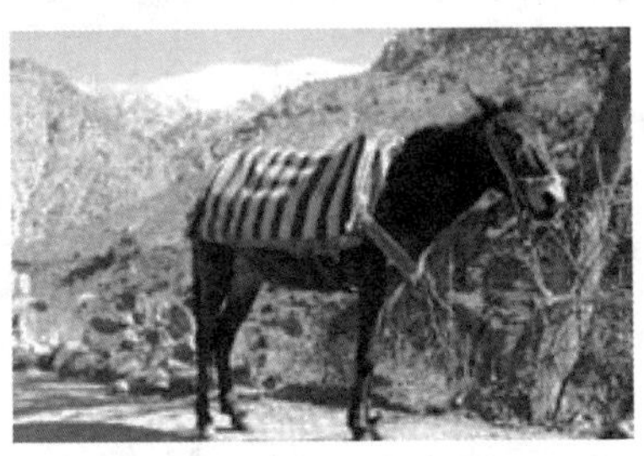

Soft focus

You can achieve a soft-focus effect using one of the following methods:

- By using a soft-focus filter or a diffuser filter.
- By using a diffuser panel or a soft-box over a light source
- By covering the front of your lens with a light-coloured nylon stocking
- By smearing Vaseline over a spare filter and attaching it to the front of the lens
- By over-exposing the shot by ½ or 1 stop.

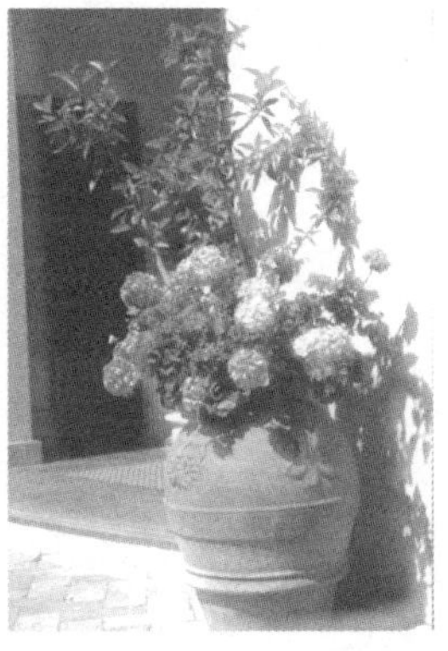

Soft focus can be useful for hiding skin blemishes in portraits.

Soft focus is good for weddings, portraits, flowers or anything that you want to give a romantic feel.

Photographic Assignments

General tips

If you don't have time for specific details then here are some general tips:

- Hold the camera steady. If you can't, then use a tripod. Make sure your subject is in focus.
- Have the sun behind you to eliminate any unwanted shadows. Outdoor photography is best done in the early morning or late afternoon/evening when the light is at its softest. 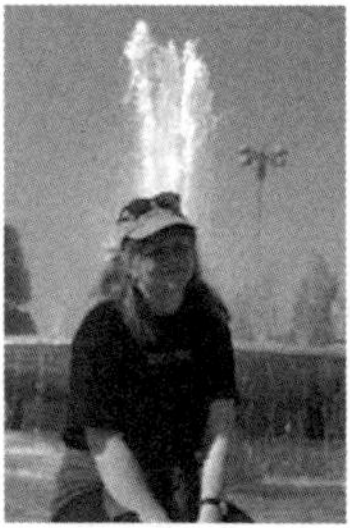
- Try to eliminate anything in your photograph that may distract away from the main subject (such as a bright red car in front of a house). The photograph here shows a common mistake – always check what appears behind the principle subject - things may appear to 'grow out' of the subject! Also make sure that people's eyes are open.
- Get closer to your subject. Try to fill the frame with it.
- Make sure you choose the best orientation – portrait or landscape.

People & Portraits

- In portraits, make sure that you focus on the eyes.

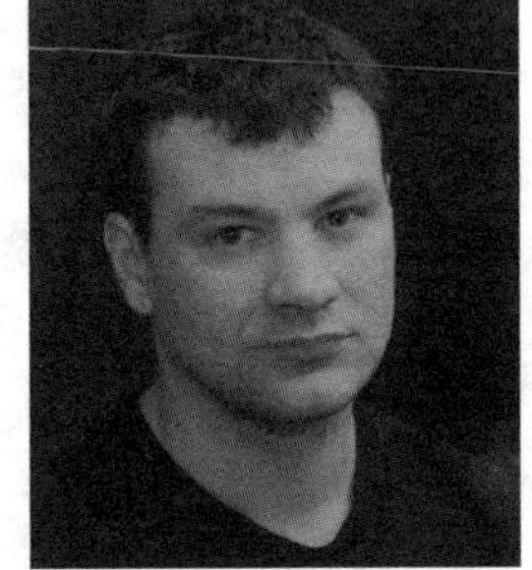

- Put the background out of focus by having a wide aperture e.g. f/5.6. Avoid clutter in front of the sitter.
- Choose a short telephoto lens with a focal length between 80mm and 135mm.
- Choose an simple background that does not distract away from the main subject.
- Try not to use the built-in flash on your camera.
- If using a flash unit bounce it off a reflector onto the subject.
- Check that there will be no reflections of the flash in windows or mirrors.
- For indoor portraits, a good lighting effect is to have one light source to light the face on the left and another light source behind the subject and to the right.

The photograph below depicts how you can set up your own makeshift portrait studio.

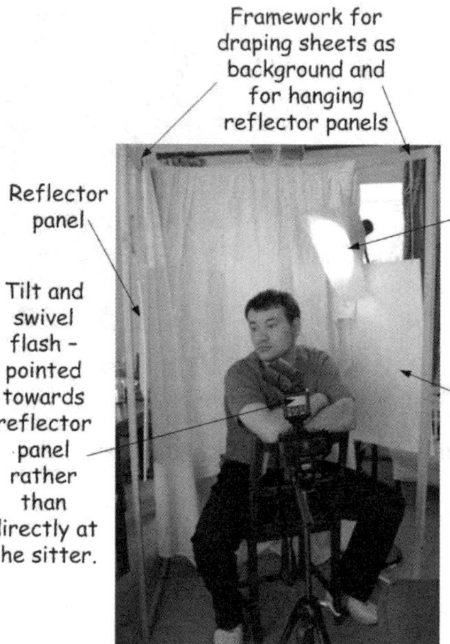

- Make sure the subject is positioned so that there is no bright light or sun shining in his or her eyes. Have the sun to one side or shoot in the shade (use fill-in flash and reflectors if required). This will also keep skin tones fresh.

- Get up close to the person – try to fill the whole frame. Head and shoulders shots are usually good though full-length shots are good when the person is involved in an activity.

- Keep the eyes sharp and in focus.

- A piece of white card or a reflector under the chin (but out of sight) will help give a flattering chin-line.

- If the person's hands are doing nothing then ask them to put them in their pockets (men) or clasp them (women).

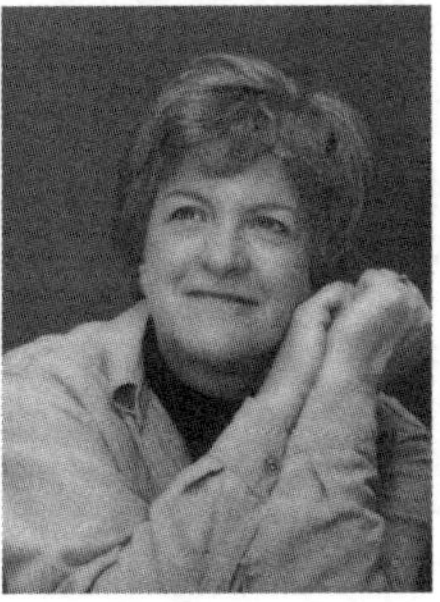

- Try having the sitter sitting at an angle to the camera, rather than head on.

- Another popular pose is the subject leaning into the camera.

- For a group photograph, ask them to bunch up together in a natural, informal way rather than in a straight line. Try to have a focal point such as a new baby or someone's birthday cake. Take a couple of photos to guarantee good expressions on all the faces.

- If the subject is wearing glasses, check for reflections. If in doubt, ask the sitter to tilt their head just slightly downwards.

- Double chins – shoot from above, with the head upwards.

- Wrinkles – use a soft diffused light or a soft focus filter.

- Expressive eyes – hold the head down, with the eyes looking upwards.

- Not much hair – shoot from below.

Children

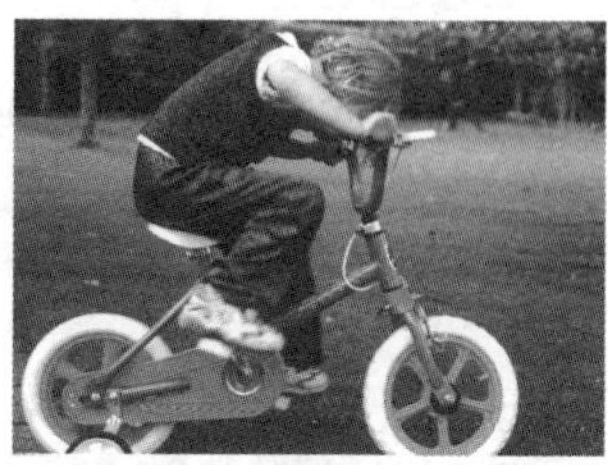

- Photograph children unposed, if possible.
- Crouch down to their level. Get in close.
- If posed for a portrait, give them something like sticky tape to play with. It takes their mind off the fact that they are having their picture taken!
- Don't use the built-in flash directly on the child – they are more susceptible to red-eye. Use a flash with an adjustable head, which you can point at a reflective surface to bounce the light.
- Don't be afraid of photographing children as they are crying or having a tantrum. It is very photogenic!
- Remember children have about a 10-minute attention span for posing for photographs.
- Try to make it fun. Turn a photo session into a day out at the funfair, for example – this way everyone will be satisfied!

Babies

- For babies use a soft light to emphasise their rounded features.
- Prop babies up in a chair rather than have them lying down.
- Distract babies with a mobile or something similar to lift their heads and create expression in their faces.
- Be prepared for that shot which can happen at a moment's notice. Have your camera ready – on a tripod preferably.

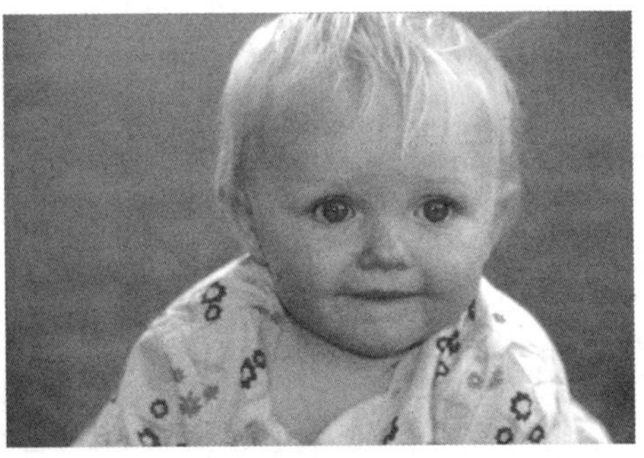

Weddings

- Get in front of the crowd and use a wide-angle lens if you are close up to the couple.
- Use films with large number of frames (e.g. 36 exp) to reduce the number of times you will need to change the film.
- Use a slow-film (e.g. ISO 100) so that enlargements do not lose too much quality.
- Try and get above the crowd, if possible, and shoot the whole gathering.
- Photograph the guests *after* the ceremony – they are far more relaxed.
- For photographs of the married couple, keep the background simple and out of focus (use a large aperture e.g. f/5.6).
- Use a soft-filter for shots of the married couple for a romantic feel to the photograph.
- Take as many unusual shots of the ceremony as possible (such as a group of guests chatting) rather than imitating what the official photographer is doing. The married couple will be grateful for these 'natural' shots, which they themselves never saw.

Landscapes

- For landscapes use a lens with a short focal length (wide angle lens) say 28mm to 35mm, so that you get plenty of the landscape in the photograph.

- Landscapes should be sharp from front to back so you need to have a large depth of field by using a small aperture e.g. f/16 or higher.

- A small aperture may result in a longer exposure, so use a tripod to reduce the effect of camera shake.

- Use slow speed film e.g. ISO 50-100 for its fine grain to enhance rich colours.

- Focus one third of the way into the subject. This is the optimum position (hyperfocal distance) for ensuring the depth of field covers as much of the scene as possible.

Focus one third into the scene

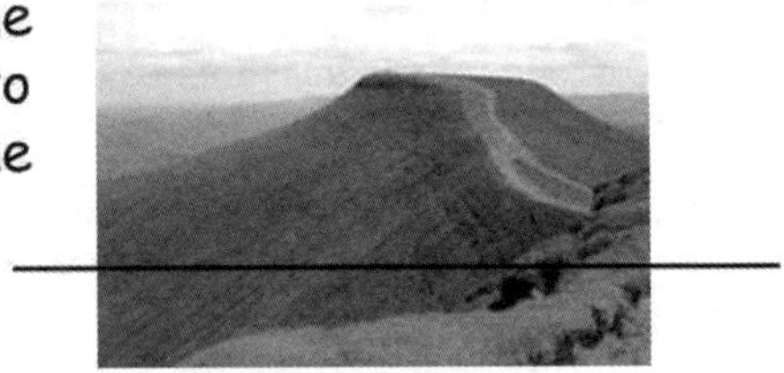

- Try to take your photograph in the early morning or late afternoon/evening. The low sun creates long shadows and a warming effect. Mid-day sun can create harsh lighting effects. In the very early morning the light is at its 'softest'. You'll be alone too, without other human distraction!

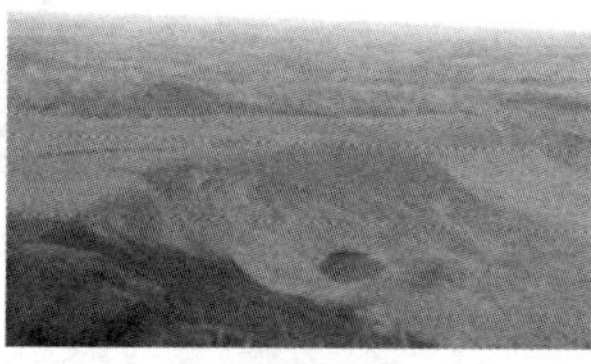

- Try the 'Rule of Thirds' (page 90) and place an object of interest one third of the way up the scene from the bottom.

- Try using black and white film for dramatic landscapes.

- For sunrises and sunsets, use a warm-up filter.

- Use a neutral density graduate filter – it darkens the top part (the sky) so that it requires the same exposure as the rest of the photograph.

- For a creative effect, try contra-jour – this involves shooting into the light (at sunset and sunrise) to produce silhouettes. But watch out for glare.

- Include some foreground detail to 'Lead the Eye' (page 93) from the front to the back of the scene e.g. a path, a river or rocks.

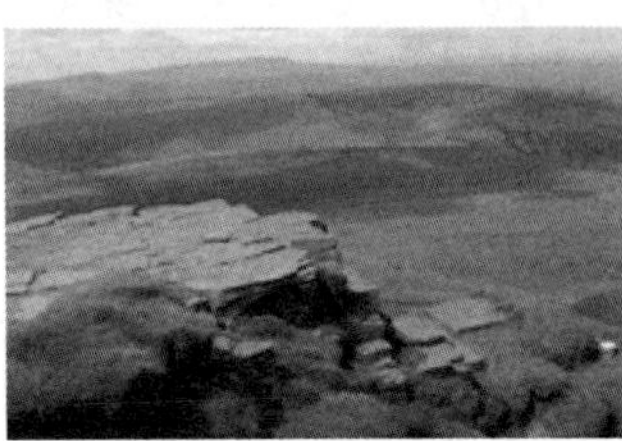

- Try to eliminate distracting features such as cars and litter.

- Try the portrait /up-right orientation as well as the traditional landscape view.

- Keep the sun at 90 degrees to the camera.

- Walk around for the best view - don't just take it where you are. Also try out the view from a crouching position or high up on a wall.

- Try using a polarising filter - it's the most useful filter for landscapes. It deepens the sky and reduces glare on foliage.

Skylines

- Photographs of the sky should be taken in context – place land, sea or buildings for example, in the foreground.
- Create dramatic skylines by having the horizon low in the frame. Use the 'Rule of Thirds' (page 90).

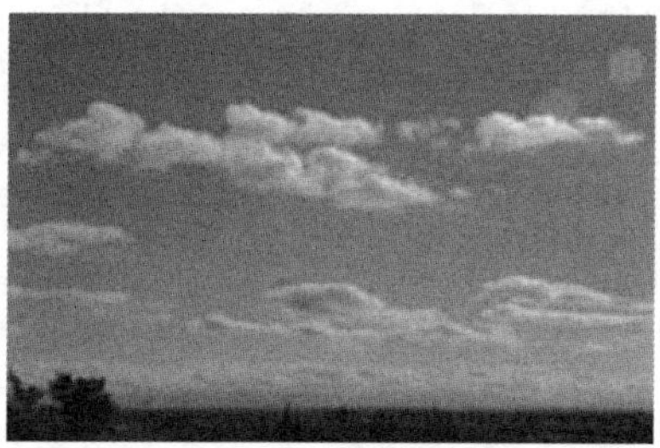

- Expose for the brightest part of the sky to create richer colours and emphasise the colours and shapes in the sky.
- Use a polarising filter to create a greater contrast between the sky and the clouds.
- Make sure the horizon is horizontal!

Trees & Woods

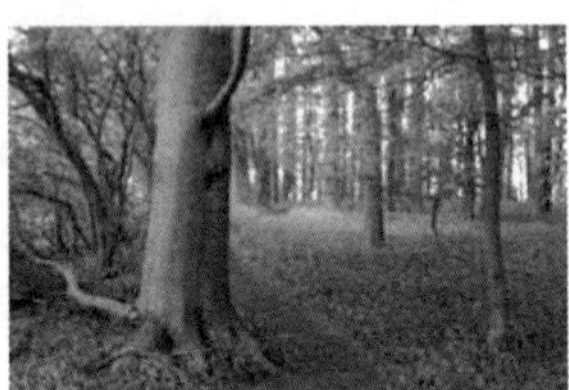

- In woods use a polariser filter to enhance the colours of trees and plants and to reduce glare.

- Check the exposure on sunny days, as the light contrast in woods can be high. Expose for a mid-tone or use bracketing (page 94).

- Do not use a wide angle or standard lens as these will make you tilt the camera upwards, giving the effect that the trees are falling over backwards (converging verticals). Unless you have a tilt-shift lens, use a telephoto lens and shoot from a distance.

- The colours of the foliage on trees during the autumn months can be spectacular. Use slow-speed films, as they are higher in contrast and have good colour saturation.

- If it is cloudy or overcast, it may be better to use a warm filter to brighten up the duller colours.

- Try photographing early or late in the day, as the light is warmer.

Caves & Caverns

- There are many caves and caverns around the world with amazing stalagmites and stalactites, often in a variety of colours. Getting enough light is your main concern here. Built-in flashes, and even flash attachments, are often not enough to light up a whole cavern. They are adequate for close-ups.

- Use very fast film (ISO 1000 or 1600) so that you can get sharp pictures in these low light conditions. You will not probably be allowed to take a tripod so all shots will be handheld.

- If you can use a tripod and take lighting equipment, then, on shooting, keep your shutter open in the B-setting and fire your flash multiple times to light up the whole cavern. As this takes some experimentation, you should bracket and take many shots with different lighting arrangements.

- Use a blue '80' series filter to eliminate the effects from the artificial lighting in the caverns, which can cause unnatural casts on the rocks. If you have a digital SLR you will need to set the white balance to tungsten lighting.

Reflections

- Reflections can be found in many different mediums e.g. water, metal surfaces and windows.

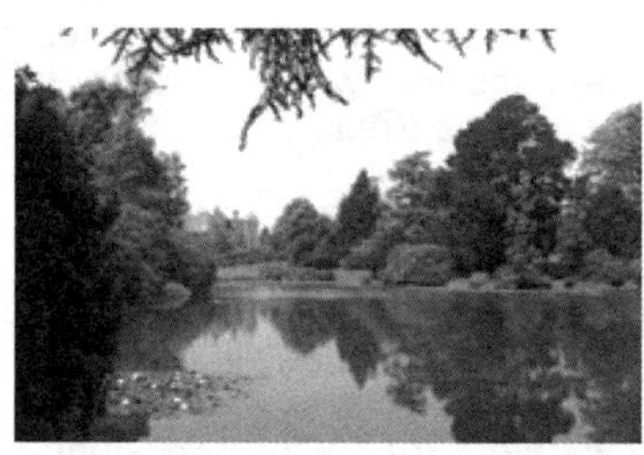

- Focus on the reflections not on the surface.
- Use a polarising filter for enhancing the reflection by removing glare from the surface.

Water

- There are several different approaches to photographing water, especially if it is moving.

- If you want to capture moving water and achieve that 'milky' white wispy effect, then you need to use a long shutter speed (about ½ second or more). The shortest shutter speed to blur water is about 1/15th second).

- If you want to freeze the motion of the water, you will need to use a faster shutter speed – about 1/250th to 1/1000th second depending on the speed of the moving water.

- Water is highly reflective, so photographing a large body of water requires overexposing by one or more stops.

- Use a polarising filter to remove the glare from water on sunny days.

- Try not to photograph water on its own. Give it some context, such as a riverbank, the beach or a boat.

Waterfalls

- For waterfalls, use a slow film (ISO 50-100). You must use a tripod.

- Use a neutral density filter/polarising filter if there is too much light around.

- To create a wispy effect on the falling water, use a long shutter speed - anything over half a second. Overexpose by +1 or +2 stops.

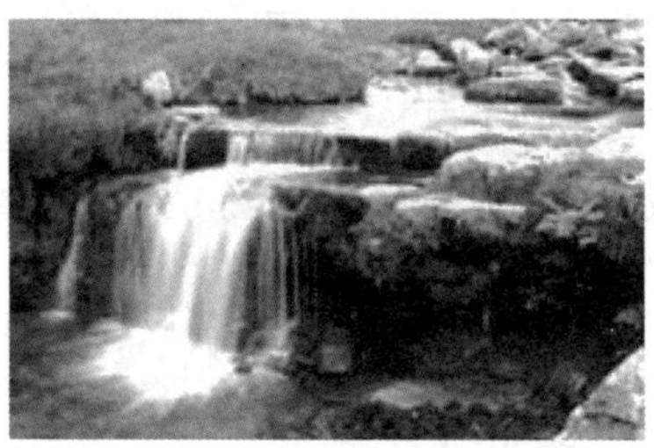

- Use a wide-angle lens and a small aperture e.g. f/22.

- Take the photograph on a dull day so there is no harsh lighting to deal with.

Plants & Flowers

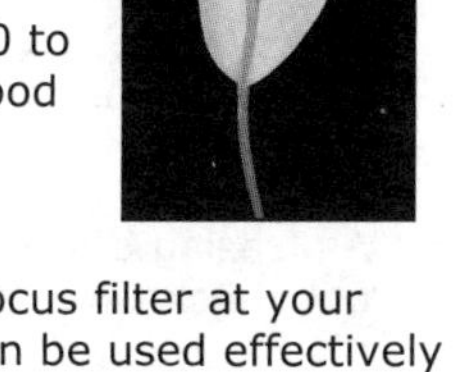

- Do not take photographs of imperfect or damaged plants or flowers. Check for any hairs, dirt or insects on the flowers as these can show up afterwards.

- Use a slow film e.g. ISO 100 to create sharp images with good colour saturation.

- Have a warm-up filter, a polarising filter and a soft-focus filter at your disposal as each of these can be used effectively in flower photography.

- Use a wide aperture e.g. f/4.0 or f/5.6 for a shallow depth of field. This ensures that only the plant is in focus and the background thrown out of focus. If you have a depth-of-field preview on your camera then you should use this to check exactly what will be in focus and what won't be.

- The background to your plant or flower is very important – it should not have any distracting features in it. A simple green background works well with most flowers. Alternatively you could shoot a flower from below, if possible, so that it is against a blue sky.

- In the outdoors a soft lighting often works well with flowers . If the light is harsh then use a white reflecting sheet to fill in any shadows. Use a fill-in flash as a last resort as it can create an artificial look.

- If it is windy, use a windshield to keep flowers still – such as white card. It can also act as a reflector.

- A pleasing effect is to spray flowers with water, but check what is being reflected in the droplets!

- In most cases flowers look good if lit from the side with a reflector to fill in shadows. However most flowers can look good if they are backlit. Textured leaves benefit from side lighting.

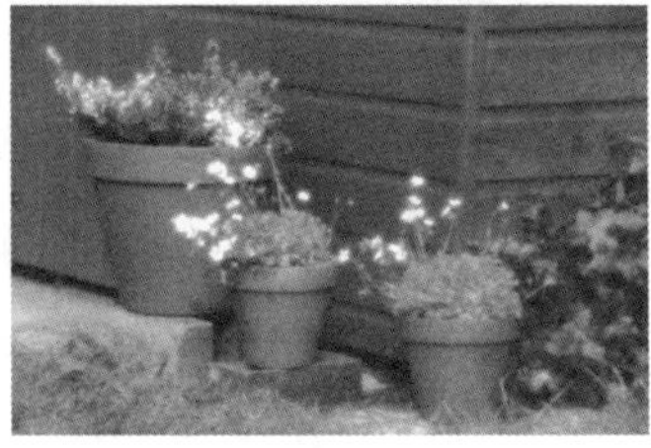

- Remember that close-up shots have a reduced depth of field. This will force you to use low shutter speeds or fast film. Use a tripod or achieve higher shutter speeds by using a flash to good effect.

Wildlife

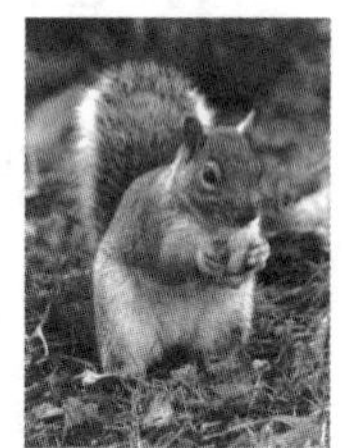

- For wildlife shots, get to know the habits of the animal or bird that you are photographing, and be in the right place at the right time. Most animals are active in the early morning and just before sunset.
- Consider a hide – natural (such as a bush) or artificial (such as a car). Animals cannot count, so if two people enter a hide and one leaves then the animal assumes no one is left!
- The nearer eye of the subject needs to be sharp. Use a telephoto lens on a tripod and use a wide aperture to maximise the shutter speed. It also has the benefit of putting the background out of focus.

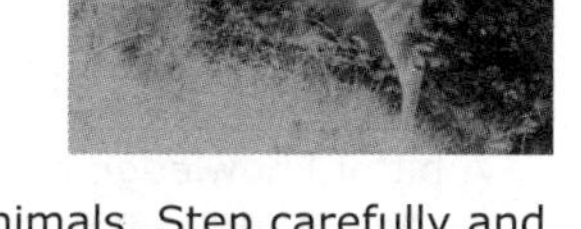

- For wild animals try not to use green grass as a background as it can make the animal appear domesticated.
- Bright clothing and pale faces can scare animals. Step carefully and quietly.

Wildlife – On Safari

- On safari take as little equipment as necessary as the conditions within the jeep won't necessarily allow you to fiddle around with lots of bits and pieces. Make sure your camera is protected at all times. Take a spare battery.

- The safaris generally take place in the early morning and late afternoon, so you will have a soft light, which is good for photography. You may want to take a polarising filter or a warm-up filter (81A) to add colour and warmth to your photos. Choose slow film – ISO 100 to capture sharp images in the sunny weather. Take a lens hood to reduce flare from the sun.

- A zoom lens with a good focal length range say 35-300mm is best for you to capture both the animals that come close as well as those in the distance.

- To reduce camera shake, take a small beanbag for your camera to rest on the windowsill of the jeep. There may not be much room for tripods. Try to shoot your subject at its level or from below. Research the animals you will be seeing. A bit of knowledge of their behaviour can really help in setting up photographs. Try to photograph the less popular animals too.

- Make sure you focus on the animal's eyes. These need to be in sharp focus.

- Try to keep the background simple – one way is to use a longer lens and wide aperture to put the background out of focus.

Birds

If you are serious about bird photography then you must invest in a lens with a long focal length – a 400mm telephoto lens is adequate but the longer the focal length the better. Using a lens with a shorter focal length will not allow you to take close-up photographs of birds, unless the birds are in captivity. Wild birds are very difficult to approach without scaring them, so using a long focal length lens and make use of a hide, if one is available.

Capturing a bird in flight is very difficult. Try to predict their flight path and make sure they are flying towards you rather than away from you.

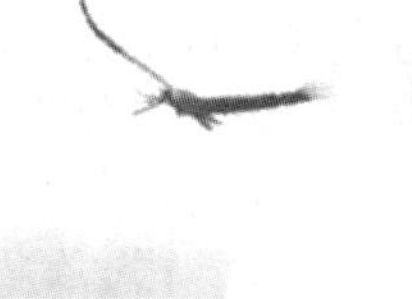

Use the aperture priority mode and choose a wide aperture to maximise the shutter speed.

Zoos & Parks

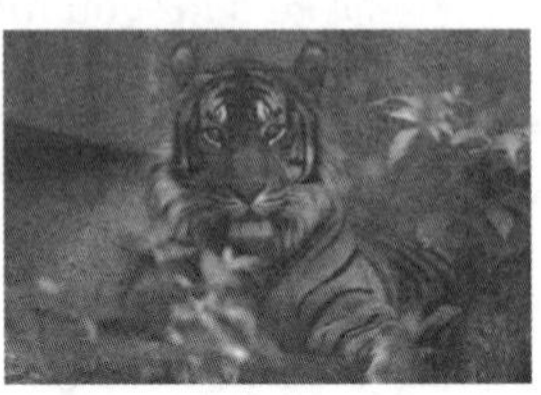

- In zoos and parks, to eliminate the wire of the cage use a wide aperture and stand as far away as possible so that the depth of field will render it invisible. Move around so that the background looks as natural as possible. The concrete background in the photograph above was inevitable as the tiger was resting. Getting the tiger to look straight into the camera was an added bonus!

- With a glass cage, go right up to the glass (at 90^0) to eliminate reflections. Ideally you want to create a dark tent around the camera and your head to reduce reflections.

- If the animals are lying down, be patient and wait until they awake and sit up.

- In the safari park where windows need to be kept closed, get the camera right up to the glass (but not touching). Try to have the car engine switched off to reduce camera shake.

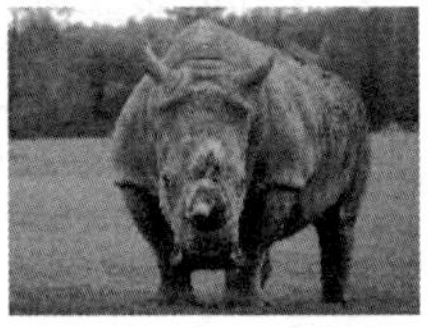

Pets

- You must get the owner's permission before taking a photograph of their pet.

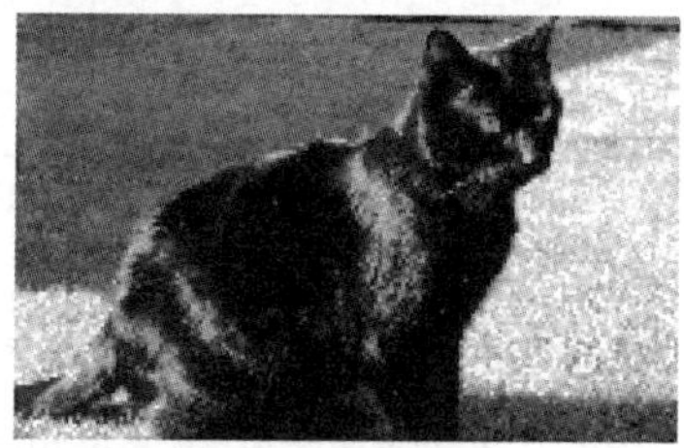

- Try to get an assistant to keep the pet interested. Give it a toy to play with.
- Try to take the photograph of the pet with the owner.
- Do not scare or distress the animal, such as using a flash.
- Crouch down to the level of the animal. Try to fill the whole frame.

Travel

- Do not take too much equipment – just take what you need in one bag. The more you take the more you will have to carry and the more that could get stolen.

- Research your travel destination so that you take the equipment relevant to the area and climate. For example, use slow films in bright, sunny places. If the photographs are going to be primarily of landscapes then make sure you have a wide-angle lens or a zoom lens that ranges from the wide-angle focal length.

- Be aware of local customs and be careful to not offend the local people. It *can* be offensive to point a camera in someone's direction – try shooting at waist level – takes practice, but you may actually get some very unique shots. If in doubt, ask permission before you take photographs and have some spare change ready.

- Don't just take standard 'postcard' photographs of the famous landmarks. Try a different angle or with some interesting foreground detail.

- Don't be afraid to take lots of photographs – you may not be visiting this place again in your lifetime!

Buildings

- Take your time with photographs of buildings. Get the right conditions. You have the luxury of your subject staying very still, day after day!

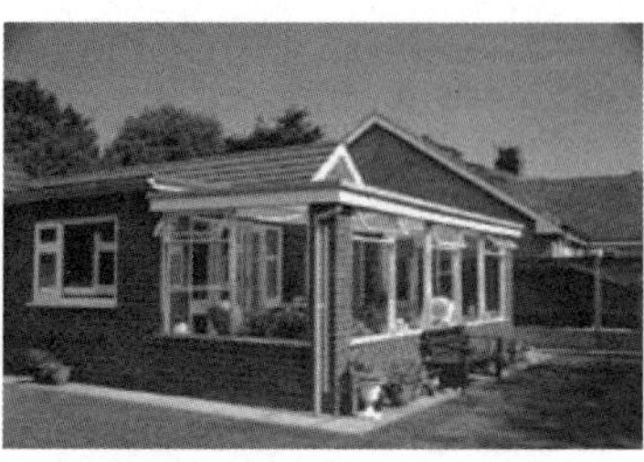

- Use a wide-angle lens e.g. 28mm to 35mm.
- To stop buildings appearing to be falling over backwards, known as 'converging verticals' or 'convergence' (due to the camera's film plane not being parallel to the plane of the subject), find a high viewpoint of the building, so you are right angles to it. Do not tilt your camera up. A tilt-shift lens will resolve this problem (page 68).
- Use a polarising filter to deepen the colours of buildings, remove reflections from windows and darken the sky around it.
- On red brickwork, a warm filter will make the buildings glow.

- Take the shot when the sun is low in the sky (early morning or late afternoon) for a warmer light.
- To eliminate people walking around a building, use a neutral density filter and a time exposure (15-30 seconds). The movement of the people will not be recorded or be very blurred.
- Try not to have cars around the building as they can distract away from the main subject.

Room interiors

- The problem with photographing room interiors is getting enough light. You must use a tripod since you may be forced to use a low shutter speed.

- You can use a flash, though you must use a reflector to reflect the bounced light into the room.

- Do not mix light – use either natural light and long exposures or artificial light.

- Use the '80' series blue filters to reduce the cast from tungsten lighting on daylight-balanced film. Alternatively you can use tungsten-balanced colour film. Use a pale magenta filter to reduce the cast from fluorescent lighting.

- If you are using a digital SLR then set your white balance parameter settings appropriately, depending on the types of light sources (the fluorescent setting or the tungsten setting).

- Avoid including windows, as the differences in brightness are too great. If a window must be included then expose for the interior.

- If the room is small use a wide-angle lens (20-28mm) and get into a corner. Try to include a mirror to give extra depth (but make sure you are not reflected in it!).
- Do not tilt the camera up, as it will create converging vertical lines.
- To make a room look bigger shoot with a wide angle from below waist level from the corner of the room.
- Don't have a cluttered foreground – open space is better and will lead the eye into the room.
- If the outside view is important, then shoot on an overcast day so that the light is soft.
- Try shooting from outside through a window or door.

Stained-glass windows

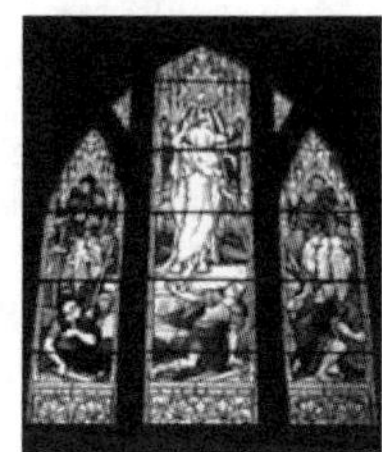

- Bright overcast days are the best for taking photographs of stained-glass windows. It softens the light and gives even illumination.

- Check if a permit is required first if you are in a religious building. Give a donation when you've finished.

- If it is possible, try to be on the same level as the window rather than pointing your camera at an upward tilt towards it.

- Use an aperture of f/8 or f/11 to keep the entire window in focus. Bracket on a range of exposures as the contrast between dark and light is vast. Use a tripod.

- Try a soft-focus for effect.

Action & Sport

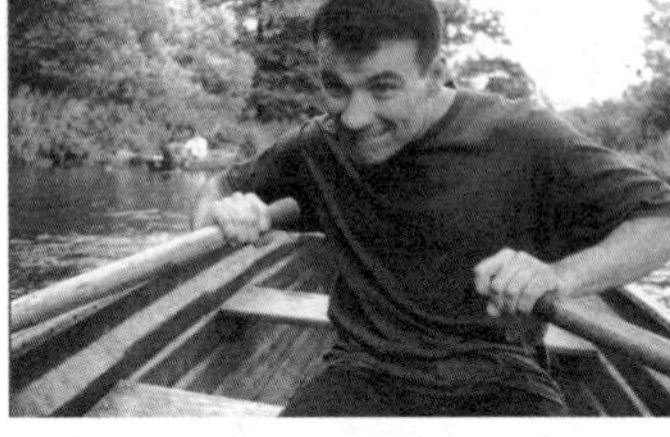

- For action shots, use a telephoto lens in the range 80-200mm.

- Use a fast shutter speed e.g. 1/500th or 1/1000th second to freeze the action with a sharp, in-focus image.

- Use a lower shutter speed if you wish to capture 'speed' with a blurring effect.

- If the subject is moving from left to right, try the 'Rule of Thirds' (page 90) by placing the subject one third of the way in from the left.

- Setting to manual focus will save time when capturing an action shot.

- If you are at a sports event try to concentrate on one particular person or one particular area, rather than trying to capture everything. For example, have your camera focused on the area around the goal post to capture the moment when a goal is scored.

- In a team sport, try to get shots of the players bunched up together. It gives a better sense of action.

- If taking a shot of a player with a ball, try to shoot just after the ball has been hit.

- Predict the behaviour of the action, such as an aircraft taking off, and set the camera up accordingly (in the right place, using manual focus, with the aperture/shutter speed as you want it).

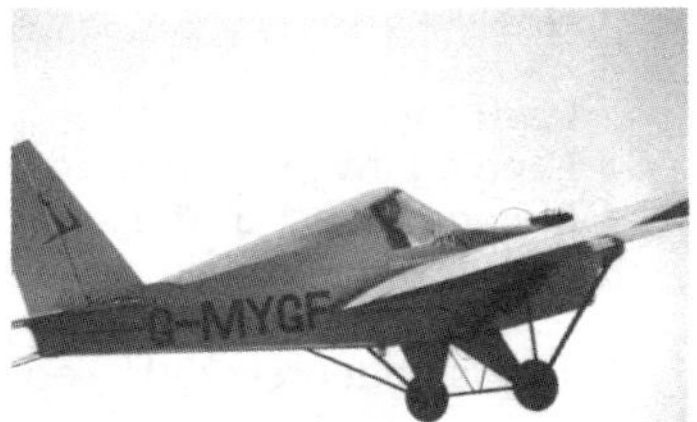

- If you are at a sporting event, note where the professional photographers are sitting and try to move in close to them if possible. They will have found the best position.

- Try a wide-angle lens to capture a group e.g. marathon runners.

- A UV filter on your lens will protect it against any dust or dirt that the action you are shooting may throw up. A screw-on filter is best – you can leave it on there permanently as a lens protector.

- Fast film ISO 400-1000 is best for low-light conditions, such as a winter's day football match. It will enable you to get fast shutter speeds.

Panning

Panning involves moving the camera with the moving object at the same speed – track it in the viewfinder. Trip the shutter whilst moving.

- Use about 1/250th second shutter speed.

- The result is the moving object appearing as a sharp image with a blurred streaky background.

- It takes practice!

Still Life

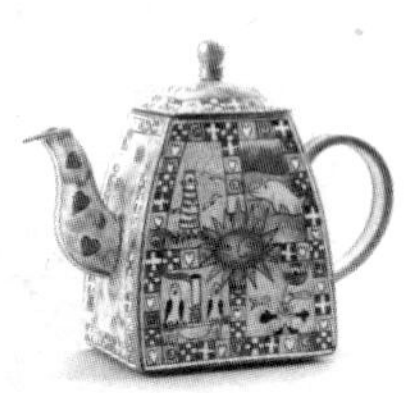

- Still life is the art of creating compositions of stationary objects.
- Take your time! The composition is the most important aspect of still life shots. Spending time getting it 'just right' is time well spent.
- Use a tripod.
- Use a lens with a focal length in the range 50 to 100mm. Try to throw as much of the background *out of focus* and keep as much of the object *in focus*.
- Reflectors are essential for controlling how the light falls on the subject. Try to eliminate harsh shadows.
- Check for dust and fluff, as they will stick out like a sore thumb in the final print.
- Try overlapping objects or cropping an object at the edges for effect.

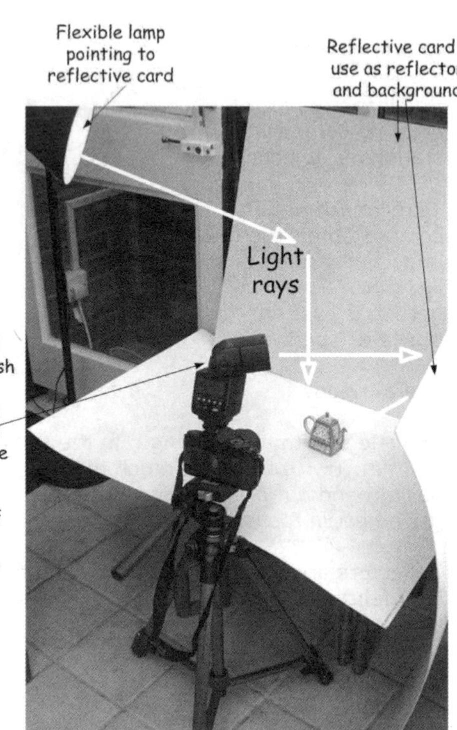

<u>Equipment for a still-life photograph</u>

- Choose a theme – similar colours, similar shapes or similar objects.

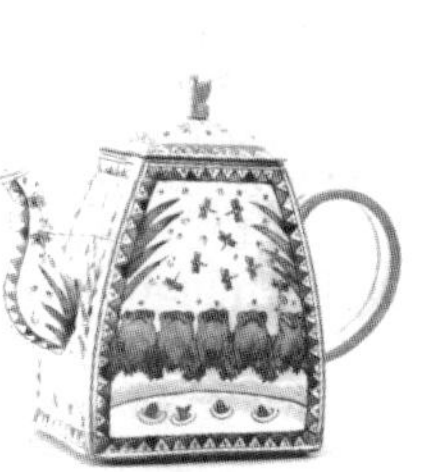

- Build up a stock of different backgrounds – card and material. Choose a suitable background that is not too fussy.

- Try not to clutter the still-life composition with too many objects.

- Try applying the 'Rule of Thirds' (page 90), though centralising works well too.

- Use black matt cards either side of a coloured object to bring out its edges against a pale background.

- 'Scoop' is the effect of 'infinite background' by using plastic glass/Formica, which curves up behind the object. It gives the effect of the object floating in air, like that used in many catalogues.

- Try using natural light (such as at a window) – if shadows are too harsh, use a reflector opposite the window to reflect the light back and eliminate any harsh shadows.

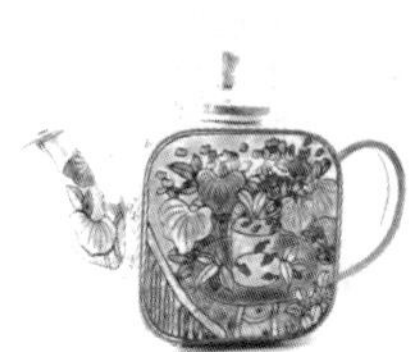

- Take a number of shots in different lighting conditions. Bracket over a range of exposure stops.

- Black and white film can be more dramatic than colour.

- Try backlighting objects by placing them on a light-box.

- With shiny objects, point the camera through black card (with a hole in it for the camera lens), so that no reflection of the camera is made in the object.

Close-ups

- A close-up picture is one where the subject is represented on film as somewhere between 1/10th (1:10 or 0.1X) of its size to life-size (1:1 or 1.0X). At greater magnifications a microscope would be required.

- There are a number of different pieces of equipment that can be used for close-up photography:

  Macro lens (close-up lens)
  Extension tubes
  Close-up filter

- Use a tripod and cable release/remote switch as camera movement is greatly magnified in close-ups.

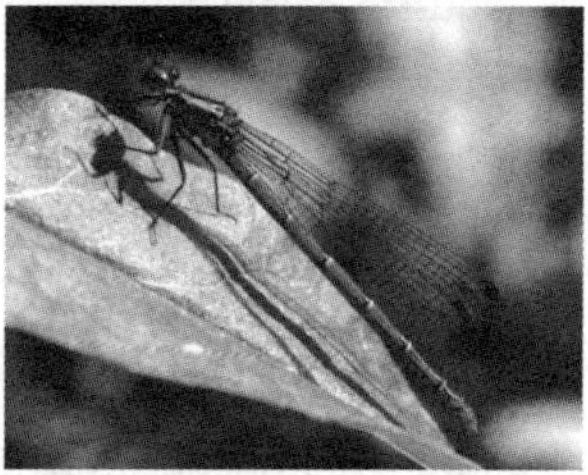

- You need to have as much of the subject in focus, keeping the distance background out-of-focus. If a subject has significant 'depth', such as the damselfly here, then try photographing it *side-on* where the depth of field will be shallower and easier to achieve.

- Remove as much dust and dirt from the subject as possible as these will be magnified in close-ups and spoil the photograph.

- For nature close-ups use a reflector (a white board will do) at the dark side of the subject to reflect any light onto it. Use the board close-up to the subject for a stronger effect. Use diffuse lighting or a diffuser panel to eliminate harsh shadows.

- Try using a polarising filter to remove any unwanted glare that is exaggerated in close-ups.

- If your camera has the facility, use mirror-lockup, as it will reduce camera shake during shutter release.

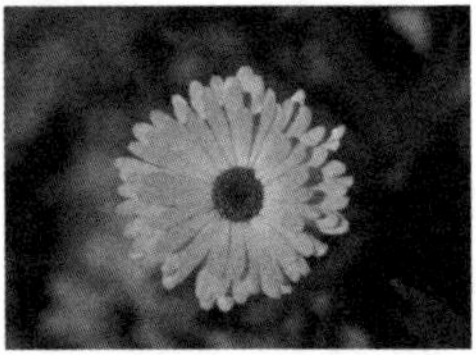

- Use a slow, fine-grained film and ensure a pin-sharp focus.

- For very small objects, the camera can be so close that it blocks out light. Use pocket mirrors or spoons as reflectors. Using a flash can be particularly useful where small apertures would normally need long shutter speeds, which can lead to camera shake.

Night-time

- The best night-time shots are just after sunset when there is still some colour in the sky.
- As there is not much light around during night-time shots, you will have to use long exposures (low shutter speed) – in the region of seconds rather than fractions of seconds.
- Use a tripod.
- Use the B-setting on your camera if required – the shutter stays open for a long as the shutter button is depressed – use a cable release to prevent unwanted camera shake.
- The photograph below shows the effect of a long exposure (approx. 20 seconds) on a busy road at night. The lights (headlights and brake lights) of the cars are shown as long streaks along the road.

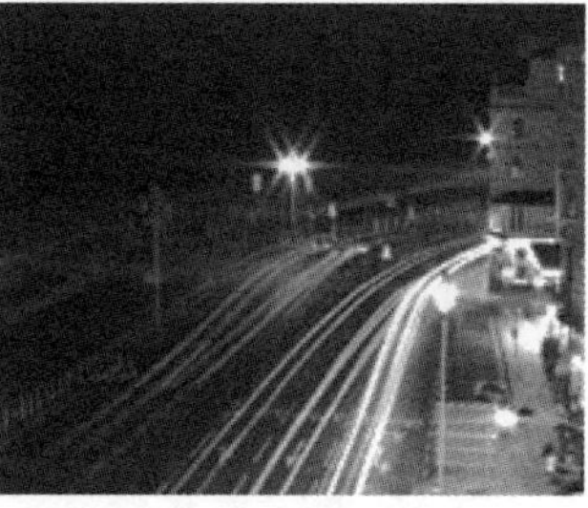

Fireworks

- In fireworks photography the most important accessory is the tripod as you may be using shutter speeds from anything between 2 and 30 seconds. A cable release or remote switch is also useful so that you can concentrate on the firework display and react to the bursts with greater speed. It also allows you to enjoy the fireworks rather than being stuck behind the viewfinder!
- Set the lens to manual focus and focus to infinity.
- Set the camera to bulb mode and use an aperture of f/8.
- When the firework is launched, open the shutter. Release it when the firework has finished.
- To capture several fireworks on one photograph: Use a piece of black card to place over the lens between fireworks (whilst the shutter is open).

Lightning

- Although lightning is one of the fastest moving subjects you will photograph, you will need a slow shutter speed.

- Use a tripod with the camera aimed at the area of the sky where the lightning is taking place. Choose a focal length that ensures some of the ground or buildings will be included. This will give it some context.

- Focus on infinity and use the bulb setting. Use an aperture of about f/5.6 or f/8 with a film speed of ISO 100.

- When taking the picture open the shutter and allow one or two lightning flashes to occur then close it. Do not allow too many lightning flashes to occur, as this will clutter your image.

- Use a cable release if you have one.

- Experiment with a number of shots using varying shutter speeds - from just a few seconds to twenty seconds. You can even leave the shutter open for several minutes whilst you wait for the lightning flashes.

The Moon

- The Moon is probably the most distant object you will ever photograph, so a long lens and a tripod are essential. A lens with a 300mm focal length is probably about right (200mm would be the minimum recommended and 500mm would record very good detail).

- Black and white film is favourable and will give good effect (you do not expect to record any colour anyway).

- The picture you are taking is essentially a bright, white object against a black sky so use the manual settings on your camera so that you can override the exposure.

- Bracket – take a few shots at differing exposures.

- If your shot is of the full moon only, the 'Luney 11' rule suggests that you should use an aperture of f/11 and a shutter speed roughly equal to the ISO of your film. So if you are using an ISO 100 film then set your camera at f/11 and a 1/125th second shutter speed.

Gravestones & Statues

- For gravestones and statues, try using black and white film as this may create the mood you are trying to portray with the shot. Use a warm-up filer to increase contrast and a polarising filter to reduce glare.

- Take the shot in good lighting, as this will highlight the stone's features and inscriptions. A reflector/diffuser can be useful to reflect a softer light onto the stone.

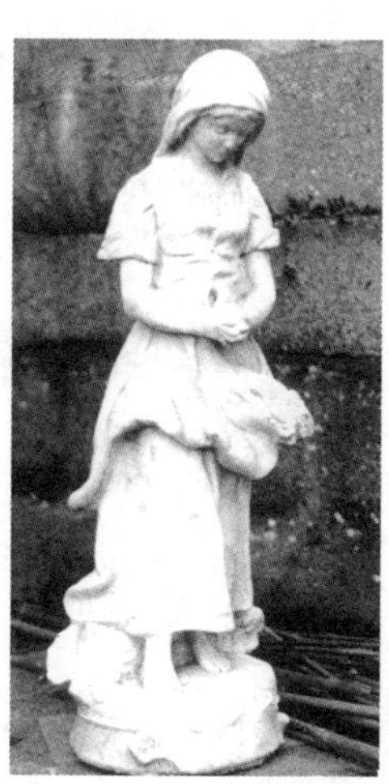

- Throw the background out of focus by using a large aperture e.g. f/5.6. Take the shot at the same level as the stone/statue – may involve crouching down or using a low tripod.

Sunsets

- The best time to capture a sunset is when the sun is just about to touch the horizon and also the afterglow after the sun has set (10-30 minutes later).

- Use a warm-up, violet or a sunset graduate filter to increase the level of warmth.

- Include some foreground detail. Try water in the foreground for a reflection of the sun, for example.

- Expose for in a part of the sky that is of average brightness.

- Use a slow film e.g. ISO 100 for better colour saturation.

- Avoid flare by keeping your lens clean. Use a lens hood if you have one. Use a tripod.

- If the foreground is not to be silhouetted (page 91) then expose for the foreground and use a graduated neutral density filter.

- Use bracketing if you are in doubt with exposures.

- Never look directly at the sun with the naked eye or through the camera viewfinder.

Aerial photography

- Aerial photography is photography of the ground taken from the air.

- Switch to manual focus and focus on infinity. Shoot at about 1/500th second.

- Use a wide aperture to keep the shutter speed high e.g. f/4. As you have focussed on infinity you will still get a good depth of field even at this aperture.

- Try to take a picture of an interesting feature rather than a 2-D shot of bare land. Take the photo at an angle to the land rather than directly downwards.

Rain, Mist & Fog

- Overcast days can sometimes be the best times to shoot landscapes or trees and foliage. Use a polarising filter to deepen colours in overcast situations and to cut through the glare that can appear on wet foliage.
  Use a neutral density filter to darken skies.
  Overexpose by + ½ or +1 stops if the light has deteriorated.

- Mist and fog often occur early in the morning, so expect to rise early to capture these effects. Mist is often more pronounced after a warm day and a cool night. A long exposure is needed so use a tripod. Use a warm-up filter ('81' series) and over-expose by ½ or 1 stops. Alternatively, to give a blue tint use an '80' series blue filter.

- For rainbows, try to time the shot so that the rainbow stands out against a dark sky or shady hill. Use a wide-angle lens to capture the whole bow. Use a polarising filter to deepen the colours of the rainbow, or under-expose by ½ stop to encourage deepening of the colours.

Concerts & Festivals

- There are few restrictions on outdoor concerts and festivals, so move in close to the performers.

- Close-up shots of the performers are generally more interesting than shots of the whole stage.

- Capture emotion on the performers face and exaggerated body movements.

- Shoot at an angle rather than head on.

- Consider shots of the crowds too.

- As the venues for indoor concerts are dark, use a fast film, such as ISO 1000. This will allow exposures of 1/125th to 1/250th second at the widest aperture.
  Do not use a flash as it may distract the performer. Take a photograph during loud passages (such as clapping) so that your camera click does not distract anyone.

Black & White photography

- You need to think about your subject differently – in black and white! Think about the form, texture or emotion, rather than the colours.

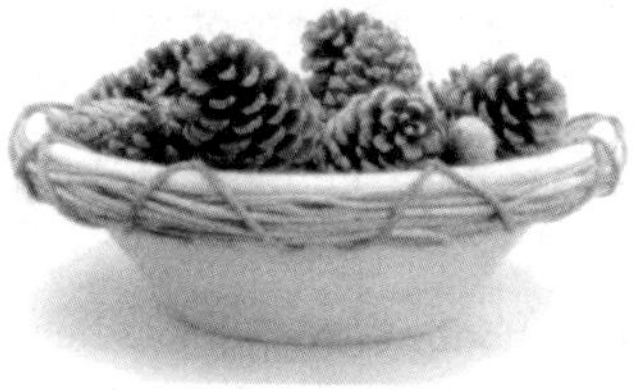

- Use black and white when you want the emphasis to be placed on emotional aspects of the scene, such as in weddings or photojournalism.

- Use black and white when you want the texture or shape of an object to be emphasised, such as a close-up of a leaf.

- Portraits, landscapes and stormy skies can look particularly good in black and white.

- Expose for mid-tones when the image has a full range of detail and tone from white to black.

Some colours appear the same shade of grey in black and white photographs - especially red and green. By using a filter you can lighten one of the colours and darken the other to bring out their differences.

Red filters

Red filters will lighten red colours and darken the green colours. Use for creating dramatic skies.

Green filters

Green filters lighten green and darken the red colours. Use in landscapes to emphasise the different shades of green.

Orange/Yellow filters

Orange and yellow filters will make a blue sky darker and the white clouds stand out.

With digital photography you will be able to convert, very easily, any colour photograph to a black and white photograph using computer software. For this reason don't use the Black and White option on your camera, if it has one.

INDEX

'80' SERIES · 76, 135, 154
'81' SERIES · 75, 154
'82' SERIES · 75
'85' SERIES · 76

A

ACTION · 138
ADOBE 1998 · 62
AE LOCK · 43, 91
AERIAL PHOTOGRAPHY · 153
AMBIENT LIGHT · 45
AMERICAN STANDARDS ASSOCIATION · 32
ANGLE OF VIEW · 25
ANIMALS · 127, 131
APERTURE · 27
ASA · 32
AUTOMATIC EXPOSURE · 34
AUTOMATIC EXPOSURE · 35
AUTUMN · 120

B

B (BULB) SETTING · 29
BABIES · 114
BACKGROUND · 87
BACKLIGHTING · 45
BIRDS · 129

BLACK AND WHITE · 156
BLACK REFLECTORS · 71
BLUE FILTER · 77
BOUNCE LIGHTING · 45
BRACKETING · 37
BRACKETING · 94, 95
BUILDINGS · 133

C

CABLE RELEASE · 85
CAGE · 130
CAMERA OBSCURA · 5
CAVERNS · 121
CAVES · 121
CCD · 51
CENTRE SPOT FILTERS · 79
CENTRE-WEIGHTED METERING · 42
CHILDREN · 113
CLOSE-UP · 145
CLOSE-UP FILTER · 78
CLOSE-UP LENS · 78
CMOS · 51
COLOUR COMPENSATION FILTERS · 76
COLOUR CONVERSION FILTERS · 76
COLOUR CORRECTION FILTERS · 75
COLOUR FILTER · 75
COLOUR MANAGEMENT · 62
COLOUR PROCESSING · 57
COLOUR SATURATION · 102
COMPACTFLASH · 52
COMPRESSION · 52

CONVERGING VERTICALS · 133
CORRECT EXPOSURE · 39
CROWDS · 155

D

DEPTH OF FIELD · 28
DEPTH OF FOCUS · 21
DIFFRACTOR FILTERS · 79
DIFFUSE LIGHTING · 45
DIFFUSER FILTER · 79
DIFFUSERS · 71
DIGITAL DARKROOM · 60
DIGITAL SINGLE LENS REFLEX CAMERAS · 7
DIGITAL SLR CAMERAS · 51
DOWNRATING FILM · 50

E

EVALUATIVE METERING · 42
EXIF · 58
EXPOSURE COMPENSATION · 36
EXPOSURE COMPENSATION · 36
EXPOSURE METERING · 42
EXTENSION TUBES · 80

F

FAST FILM. · 32

FESTIVALS · 155
FILL-IN FLASH · 99
FILL-IN LIGHT · 45
FILM · 47
FILM SPEED · 32
FILTERS · 72
FISH-EYE LENS · 67
FLASH · 81, 98
FLOWERS · 125
F-NUMBER · 24
FOCAL LENGTH · 22, 24, 27
FOCAL POINT · 18
FOCUS LOCK · 21
FOCUSSING POINTS · 20
FOG · 154
FOLIAGE · 120
FRAMING A PICTURE · 100

G

GLASSES · 112
GOLD REFLECTORS · 71
GRADUATE FILTER · 78
GRAVESTONES · 151
GREEN FILTER · 77

H

HISTOGRAM · 38
HYPERFOCAL · 116

I

IMAGE FORMATS · 55
IMAGE RESOLUTION · 51
IMAGE STABILISATION LENS · 68
INTERNATIONAL STANDARDS ORGANISATION · 32
ISO · 32

J

JPEG · 55

L

LANDSCAPES · 116
LASTROLITE · 70
LCD SCREEN · 15, 53
LEAD THE EYE · 93, 118, 136
LENS · 18
LENS HOOD · 82
LENS SPEED · 24
LIGHT METER · 83
LIGHT-BOX · 144
LIGHTNING · 149
LONG FOCUS LENS · 67
LOUPE · 84
LUNEY 11 RULE · 150

M

MACRO LENS · 67
MATRIX METERING · 42
MICRODRIVES · 52
MIRROR LENS · 67
MIRROR-LOCKUP · 146
MIST · 154
MOON · 150
MULTI-PATTERN METERING · 42

N

NATURAL LIGHT · 44
NEGATIVE · 48
NEUTRAL DENSITY FILTER · 78
NIGHT-TIME · 147

O

ORANGE FILTER · 77
OUTDOOR LIGHTING · 46
OVER-EXPOSED · 26
OVEREXPOSURE · 40

P

PALE MAGENTA FILTER · 135
PANNING · 140

PARKS · 130
PARTIAL METERING · 43
PET · 131
PHOTO CELLS · 51
PINHOLE CAMERA · 6
PIXELS · 51, 52
PLANTS · 125
POLARISING FILTER · 73
PORTRAITS · 109
PRIME LENS · 66

R

RAINBOW · 154
RAM · 61
RAW · 55
RED EYE · 99
RED FILTER · 77
REFLECTIONS · 71
REFLECTIONS · 122
REFLECTORS · 70
REFLEX MIRROR · 17
REMOTE SWITCH · 85
RESOLUTION · 51
RIM LIGHTING · 46
ROLL FILM · 47
ROOM INTERIORS · 135
ROUND FILTERS · 72
RULE OF THIRDS · 90

S

SAFARI · 128
SAFARI PARK · 130
SCOOP · 143
SEPIA FILTER · 77
SHARPNESS · 57
SHUTTER PRIORITY · 31
SHUTTER SPEED · 29
SIDE-LIGHTING · 46
SILHOUETTES · 91
SILVER REFLECTORS · 71
SINGLE LENS REFLEX · 13, 17
SKYLIGHT FILTER · 78
SLOW FILM · 32
SLR · 13, 17
SOFT-FOCUS FILTER · 78
SPLIT-IMAGE FOCUSSING · 19
SPORT · 138
SPORTS · 138
SPOT METERING · 43
SQUARE FILTERS · 72
SRGB · 62
STAINED-GLASS WINDOWS · 137
STANDARD LENS · 66
STAR FILTER · 79
STATUES · 151
STILL LIFE · 141
SUN · 46
SUNSET · 152

T

TELEPHOTO LENS · 66
THROUGH-THE-LENS · 17
THROUGH-THE-LENS METERING · 34
TIFF · 55
TILT AND SHIFT LENS · 68
TILT-SHIFT LENS · 133
TRANSPARENCY · 49
TRAVEL · 132
TREES · 120
TRIPOD · 69
TTL · 17
TTL-METERING · 34
TUNGSTEN FILTER · 121
TUNGSTEN LIGHT · 46

U

UNDER-EXPOSED · 26
UNDEREXPOSURE · 41
UNIPODS · 69
UPRATING FILM · 50
UV FILTER · 74

V

VIEWFINDER · 17
VIGNETTING · 79

W

WARM-UP FILTERS · 75
WATER · 123
WATERFALLS · 124
WHITE BALANCE · 56
WHITE REFLECTORS · 71
WIDE-ANGLE LENS · 66
WILDLIFE · 127
WINDOWS · 135, 137
WOODS · 120

Y

YELLOW FILTER · 77

Z

ZOOM BURST · 101
ZOOM LENS · 66
ZOOS · 130

Space for your own notes

Space for your own notes

Space for your own notes

Space for your own notes

Space for your own notes

Space for your own notes

Space for your own notes

www.littlephotobook.com